# Wings —from— Afar

## An Ecoregional Approach to Conservation of Neotropical Migratory Birds in South America

**Roberto Roca,**
**Leslie Adkins, M. Christina Wurschy,**
**Kevin L. Skerl**

The Nature Conservancy®
LATIN AMERICA
AND CARIBBEAN
DIVISION

USAID

**The Nature Conservancy**
Latin America and Caribbean Division
1814 North Lynn Street
Arlington, Virginia 22209

Roca, R., Adkins, L., Wurschy, M.C., and K.L. Skerl 1996. Wings From Afar: An Ecoregional Approach to Conservation of Neotropical Migratory Birds in South America. America Verde Publications. The Nature Conservancy, Latin America and Caribbean Division, Arlington, Virginia.

**Library of Congress Catalog Card Number:** 96-68384
**ISBN** 1-886765-03-0

**Editing:**
Norah Deakin Davis
**Illustrations and Graphic Design:**
Luis M. Ramirez
**Mapping:**
Kevin L. Skerl

Printed and Bound in the United States of America
First Edition

6 5 4 3 2 1

*America Verde*

**Publications for preservation - a series of The Nature Conservancy to enhance the capacity to preserve the biological diversity of Latin America and the Caribbean.**

# Wings
## —from—
# Afar

# Contents

8      Preface
10      Acknowledgments

## *Introduction*      *by Robert S. Ridgely*

14      Focus on Neotropical Migrants
     Objectives of the Project

## *Chapter* 1      *Approach*

18      Ecoregions
     Migratory Species and Their Status
     Migrants in Ecoregions, Nations, and Parks in Peril
     Information Management

## *Chapter* 2      *Regional Assessment*

26      Migratory Birds in South America
     Distributions in Ecoregions
     Migrants with a South American Affinity
     Species of Conservation Concern
     Refugia and Endemic Centers

**Chapter** *3*          *National Assessments*

**60**

Bolivia
Colombia
Ecuador
Paraguay
Peru
Venezuela

**Chapter** *4*          *Habitat Preferences and Threats*

**136**

Breeding Habitats
Nonbreeding Habitat Use
*Aquatic Habitats*
*Disturbed Habitats*
*Coffee, Cacao, and Citrus Plantations*
Migrant Sensitivity to Habitat Alteration
Habitat Threats

**Chapter** *5*          *The Conservation Challenge*

**152**

The Ecoregional Approach
The Plight of Neotropical Migrants
Where Do We Go from Here?
A Global Outlook

**158**          Glossary
**162**          Appendix
**165**          Literature Cited and Consulted
**174**          Endnotes

# TABLES

Table 2.1  Neotropical Migratory Birds of the Andean/Southern Cone Region: Conservation Status and Sensitivity to Habitat Alteration

Table 2.2  Ecoregions of the Andean/Southern Cone Region of South America

Table 2.3  Distribution and Conservation Status of Neotropical Migratory Birds in Andean/Southern Cone Nations and Ecoregions

Table 2.4  Distribution and Conservation Status of Neotropical Migratory Birds in Parks in Peril Sites

Table 3.1  Distribution and Conservation Status of Neotropical Migratory Birds in Bolivia

Table 3.2  Distribution and Conservation Status of Neotropical Migratory Birds in Colombia

Table 3.3  Distribution and Conservation Status of Neotropical Migratory Birds in Ecuador

Table 3.4  Distribution and Conservation Status of Neotropical Migratory Birds in Paraguay

Table 3.5  Distribution and Conservation Status of Neotropical Migratory Birds in Peru

Table 3.6  Distribution and Conservation Status of Neotropical Migratory Birds in Venezuela

Table 3.7  Parks in Peril Site Occurrences of Neotropical Migratory Birds

Table 4.1  Occurrence of Neotropical Migrants in Aquatic and Secondary Habitats within Ecoregions

# FIGURES

Figure 2.1  Ecoregions and Parks in Peril Sites of the Andean/Southern Cone Region

Figure 2.2  Species Richness in Ecoregions:  All Neotropical Migrants

Figure 2.3  Species Richness in Ecoregions:  Migrants with a South American Affinity

Figure 2.4  Species Richness in Ecoregions:  Migrants of Conservation Concern

Figure 2.5  Species Richness in Ecoregions:  Migrants of Conservation Concern with a South American Affinity

Figure 3.1  Ecoregions and Parks in Peril Sites of Bolivia

Figure 3.2  Migrant Species Richness in Ecoregions of Bolivia

Figure 3.3  Migrant Species Richness in Ecoregions of Bolivia: Species of Conservation Concern

Figure 3.4  Ecoregions and Parks in Peril Sites of Colombia

Figure 3.5  Migrant Species Richness in Ecoregions of Colombia

Figure 3.6  Migrant Species Richness in Ecoregions of Colombia: Species of Conservation Concern

Figure 3.7  Ecoregions and Parks in Peril Sites of Ecuador

Figure 3.8  Migrant Species Richness in Ecoregions of Ecuador

Figure 3.9  Migrant Species Richness in Ecoregions of Ecuador: Species of Conservation Concern

Figure 3.10 Ecoregions and Parks in Peril Sites of Paraguay

Figure 3.11 Migrant Species Richness in Ecoregions of Paraguay

Figure 3.12 Migrant Species Richness in Ecoregions of Paraguay: Species of Conservation Concern

Figure 3.13 Ecoregions and Parks in Peril Sites of Peru

Figure 3.14 Migrant Species Richness in Ecoregions of Peru

Figure 3.15 Migrant Species Richness in Ecoregions of Peru: Species of Conservation Concern

Figure 3.16 Ecoregions and Parks in Peril Sites of Venezuela

Figure 3.17 Migrant Species Richness in Ecoregions of Venezuela

Figure 3.18 Migrant Species Richness in Ecoregions of Venezuela: Species of Conservation Concern

# PREFACE

Nearly two-thirds of bird species in the United States depend on the forests and coasts of Latin America and the Caribbean to survive the North American winter. These neotropical migrants are a reminder of our responsibility to conserve the entire spectrum of habitats the birds encounter during their annual journey. They are a symbol of the ever-present prospect of a silent spring.

Until now, integrated information on the distribution of neotropical migrants was available principally for their North American breeding habitats. With the publication of *Wings from Afar: An Ecoregional Approach to Conservation of Neotropical Migratory Birds in South America*, we now have information on their winter homes as well. Analysis of these data was made possible through the use of a new, comprehensive classification scheme based on ecoregions.

Publication of this document is the culmination of a landmark effort that brought together noted ornithologists, university researchers, and leading experts from The Nature Conservancy's staff and partner organizations. Together, this group compiled the baseline information necessary to document the importance of habitats in Venezuela, Colombia, Ecuador, Peru, Bolivia, and Paraguay for neotropical migrants. Neotropical migratory birds winter in every country in South America, but these six nations provided a manageable focus for this initial study. Together, these countries make up the Andean/Southern Cone (ASC) Region, a term used by The Nature Conservancy to designate one of five administrative regions within the organization's Latin America and Caribbean Division.

The ASC Region represents an enormous variety of habitats, ranging from the paramo of the high Andes to the steamy lowland Amazonian rainforests and the dry savannas of the chaco. Since 1987, the Conservancy has been working to protect the biological diversity of these countries. The Conservancy's ASC Regional Program is supporting the

efforts of an extensive network of local conservation organizations to conserve 25 globally significant areas. More than 31 million acres are protected.

Every state in the continental United States shares neotropical migratory bird species with countries of the ASC Region. Of 406 species of birds that breed in North America and migrate to Latin America and the Caribbean, 132 species winter in the ASC Region.

It is of particular conservation interest that 53 of those species use South America as their *principal* habitat during the nonbreeding season. Unfortunately, the results of our study indicate that two-thirds of these 53 species have a tenuous future.

These findings underscore the need to intensify conservation efforts in the ASC Region. For the first time, we know where neotropical migrants are during the winter, where they are protected, and where they are threatened. This is an initial step in the process of understanding where to concentrate efforts to protect the South American habitat of neotropical migratory birds. This habitat was limited to begin with and now is fast disappearing.

We are pleased to share this ground-breaking study and trust that it will enable the Conservancy, our partner organizations, and other conservation groups to look beyond the borders of our respective countries and take the necessary steps to conserve our common natural heritage, the "wings from afar" that link our nations.

Gregory A. Miller
Vice President and Regional Director
Andean/Southern Cone Region
The Nature Conservancy

# ACKNOWLEDGMENTS

Indispensable help was provided by The Nature Conservancy's (TNC) partners in nongovernmental organizations in Latin America. Along with ornithologists and other experts, these NGO partners generously shared their knowledge, forwarded our requests for information, and helped in every way imaginable. Our fervent hope is that the results of this study will benefit our Andean/Southern Cone Region partners by focusing attention on the vital and beautiful areas in need of protection for migratory birds and all other living things.

We are deeply grateful to Robert S. Ridgely, director of the Neotropical Ornithology Center, Philadelphia Academy of Natural Sciences, who provided critiques and advice on every topic related to neotropical migratory birds in his capacity as the project's expert consultant. His expertise and amicability made him a pleasure to work with. We are also thankful to Steven Hilty, senior ornithology leader, Victor Emmanuel Tours, and a long-term consultant to the Conservancy, for his assistance in generating a preliminary list of austral migrants.

We are indebted to the vision and support of John Sawhill, president and chief executive officer of The Nature Conservancy; Geoffrey Barnard, former vice president and executive director of the Latin America and Caribbean Division; Brad Northrup, vice president and deputy director of the Latin America and Caribbean Division; Gregory Miller, vice president and regional director of the Andean/Southern Cone Region; and Kent Redford, director of Conservation Science and Stewardship, Latin America and Caribbean Division, all of the Conservancy, whose comments, support, contacts, and encouragement greatly contributed to this project.

This publication was made possible through support provided by the Office of the Environment, Bureau for Latin America and the Caribbean, U.S. Agency for International Development, under terms of Grant No. LAC-0782-A-00-0047-00. The opinions expressed herein are those of the authors and do not necessarily reflect the views of the U.S. Agency for International Development.

We thank David Pashley, national coordinator of Partners in Flight, and William Hunter, wildlife biologist - Nongame Partnerships, U.S. Fish and Wildlife Service, for their help with the plan for conservation priorities developed by the Partners in Flight consortium and Bruce Peterjohn, coordinator of the North American Breeding Bird Survey, for supplying population trends.

We are grateful to David Olson, conservation scientist, Conservation Science Program of the World Wildlife Fund, for providing geographic information system data for ecoregions and to Roger Sayre, director, Biodiversity Programs; Andrea Cristofani, Spatial Information project manager; and Stuart Sheppard, GIS assistant, of TNC's Conservation Science and Stewardship Department, for advice and support on map production. We thank Len West, director, Protected Areas Programs, and Jerry Touval, Colombia program director, both of the Andean/Southern Cone Region, for their insights and help in contacting our partners.

Several individuals were kind enough to review the book in its entirety or specific sections of the manuscript, and we are grateful for the time they spent on evaluating the book and providing additional data: Germán Andrade, director ejecutivo, Fundación Natura, Colombia; David Ewert, director of Science and Stewardship, TNC's Michigan Chapter, USA; Tarsicio Granizo, Wetlands Project coordinator, IUCN-Sur, Ecuador; Miguel Lentino, ornithologist and curator, Colección Ornitologica Phelps, Sociedad Audubon, Venezuela; Alberto Madroño, field biologist of Mbaracayu Nature Reserve, Fundación Moises Bertoni, Paraguay; J.V. Remsen, curator of Birds and adj. professor of Zoology, Louisiana State University, USA; and Pedro G. Vásquez, director tecnico, CDC Universidad Nacional Agraria la Molina, Peru. We extend special thanks to Mickey Edwards, Harvard University; William Stolzenburg, associate editor, TNC; Suzanne Aloi, fundraising coordinator, Andean/Southern Cone Region; and Jennifer Wheeler, master's student, University of Maryland, for their stylistic contributions. We are grateful to John Kerr, production coordinator, Resources, and Connie Gelb, photo editor, both of the Conservancy, for giving us access to their photographic files. Additionally, we thank the following administrative assistants of the Andean/Southern Cone Region: Adrienne Florez and Jeannette Little for their translations of texts and Marita Collins, Ana Garcia, Kimberly Hagerty, and Cristina Pratt for their assistance.

We would like especially to thank the following for their participation, interest, and invaluable data: Eduardo Velasco Abad, coordinator, Centro de Datos para la Conservación de Colombia; Paulina Arroyo, social coordinator, Fundación Antisana (FUNAN), Ecuador; Percy Bacarreza C., gerente técnico, Fondo Nacional para el Medio Ambiente (FONAMA), Bolivia; Gabriel Baracatt, director ejecutivo, Protección del Medio Ambiente-Tarija (PROMETA), Bolivia; Teodoro Bustamante, director ejecutivo, Fundación Natura, Ecuador; Chris Canaday, comisión del Consejo Ecuatoriano para la Conservación e Investigación de las Aves (CECIA); Victor Pulido Capurro, director, Programa de Conservación y Desarrollo Sostenido de Humedales (PCDH), Peru; Susan E. Davis, Museo de Historia Nacional Noel Kempff Mercado, Bolivia; Carlo Dlouhy, zoologo, Universidad Nacional de Asunción, Paraguay; Maria Luisa Urday de Escobari, gerente general, Fondo Nacional para el Medio Ambiente (FONAMA), Bolivia; Eduardo Forno, director ejecutivo, Centro de Datos para la Conservación de Bolivia; Gustavo Suarez de Freitas, director ejecutivo, ProNaturaleza, Peru; Ma. del Carmen Rocabado de Garola, gerente general, Fondo Nacional para el Medio Ambiente (FONAMA), Bolivia; Raúl Gauto, director ejecutivo, Fundación Moisés Bertoni, Paraguay; Paul Greenfield, comisión del Consejo Ecuatoriano para la Conservación e Investigación de las Aves (CECIA); Stephan Halloy, Departamento de Ciencias, Fundación Amigos de la Naturaleza (FAN), Bolivia; Floyd E. Hayes, assistant professor of Biology, Caribbean Union College, Trinidad and Tobago; Natalia Gómez Hoyos, bióloga, Corporación Centro de Datos para la Conservación de Colombia, Corporación Autónoma Regional del Cauca; Lois Jammes, Asociación Armonía, Bolivia; Maria Helena Jervis, directora ejecutiva, Fundación Antisana (FUNAN), Ecuador; Hermes Justiniano, director ejecutivo, Fundación Amigos de la Naturaleza (FAN), Bolivia; Niels Krabbe, comisión del Consejo Ecuatoriano para la Conservación e Investigación de las Aves (CECIA); Fausto López, director ejecutivo, Fundación Arcoiris, Ecuador; Alfredo Luna, director ejecutivo, Consejo Ecuatoriano para la Conservación e Investigación de las Aves (CECIA); Juan Mayr, director ejecutivo, Fundación Pro-Sierra Nevada de Santa Marta, Colombia; Charles Munn, research zoologist, International Program of the Wildlife Conservation Society, USA; Jeffrey A. Nield, technical assistant, Fundación Antisana (FUNAN), Ecuador; Rodrigo Ontaneda, presidente, Fundación Maquipucuna, Ecuador; Manuel A. Rios, director, Centro de Datos para la Conservación del Perú; Manuel La Rosa, director técnico, ProNaturaleza, Peru; Ruth Elena Ruiz, directora Biodiversidad y Areas Protegidas, Fundación Natura, Ecuador; Juan Pablo Ruíz, executive director, ECOFONDO, Colombia; Carlos Sáenz, director Estación Ecologica, Alto de Mira, Fundación Pro Sierra Nevada de Santa Marta, Colombia; Thomas S. Schulenberg, The Field Museum, USA; Xavier Silva, coordinator, Corporación Centro de Datos para la Conservación del Ecuador; Cecilia Solis, directora ejecutiva, Consejo Ecuatoriano para la Conservación e Investigación de las Aves (CECIA); Wilfrido Sosa, coordinador, Centro de Datos para la Conservación de Paraguay; Maclobio Orozco U., director general sectorial de Parques Nacionales (INPARQUES), Venezuela; Thomas Valqui, Ph.D. candidate, Bolivia; Victor Vera, director de Manejo de Areas Protegidas e Investigación Aplicada, Fundación Moises Bertoni, Paraguay; Carlos Eduardo Angel Villegas, Departamento de Biodiversidad, director, Fundacion Pró Sierra Nevada de Santa Marta, Colombia; Manuel Benjamín Vivas, director ejecutivo, Fundación Puerto Rastrojo, Colombia; and Jorje Zalles, Latin American coordinator for Hawks Aloft Worldwide, Hawk Mountain Sanctuary Association, USA.

Roberto Roca, Ph.D.
Director, Migratory Bird Initiative
Latin America and Caribbean Division
The Nature Conservancy

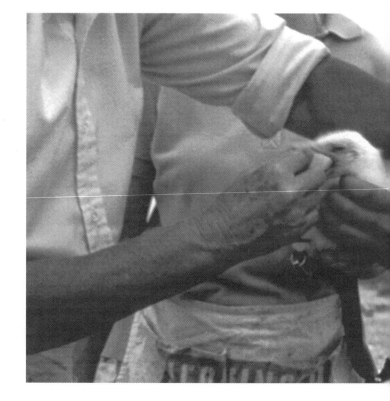

*To preserve plants, animals and natural communities that represent the diversity of life on Earth by protecting the lands and waters they need to survive.*

*— The Nature Conservancy's Mission Statement*

© Gregory Miller

# *Introduction*

## By Robert S. Ridgely

Every autumn, nature stages one of the planet's most dramatic events when approximately six billion birds make their annual journey to South America, Central America, Mexico, and the Caribbean. The only rival is the joy of their return in the spring.

During the past 200 years, humanity's impact on these avian travelers has been striking. On the North American continent and Hawaii, more than 33 species of birds have become extinct. Another 150 are in trouble. Long-term studies have clearly and tragically shown that many migratory bird populations are in decline.[1] Every state in the nation is experiencing these declines, some by as much as 75 percent.

The single most probable cause may be the loss and degradation of habitat in the neotropics. Although we have done much to alleviate the cause for the alarm sounded by Rachel Carson, this new peril threatens to silence many of these far-ranging fliers. A silent spring may yet come to pass.

Because of the mobility of migratory birds, their conservation is best addressed on large geographic and ecological scales. The Nature Conservancy's ability to work at scales that embrace landscape and ecosystem processes offers the best opportunity to understand and respond to these dramatic population declines. The Conservancy's new Migratory Bird Initiative seeks to preserve imperiled populations by protecting their most critical habitats throughout the Americas. The dwindling numbers of these birds sounds a new global challenge for the Conservancy.

Birds are universally admired for their beauty and the freedom they symbolize through their power of flight. None, however, are so admired as the long-distance migrants that mysteriously appear and disappear with the changing of the seasons. Where do they go, and how do they do it, year after year, with such unfailing accuracy? Yet, ironically, it is many of these long-distance migrants that are now recognized to be undergoing serious, long-term population declines. As part of the effort to stem this decline, the Conservancy has compiled preliminary information on the occurrence of neotropical migrants in the Andean/Southern Cone (ASC) Region of South America.

Bird migration in South America has three components. The first is the North American segment, the neotropical migrants. These birds visit South America from October to April during the northern winter.

The second component is the austral, or southern, migrants. These are the birds that fly north, staying within South America, from March to October during the southern winter. Most of the austral migrants move from temperate to tropical latitudes.

The final segment is the group of local migrants that move up and down the slopes of the Andes at varying times of the year.

For the present project, the focus was restricted to the first group: the neotropical migrants that breed in the United States and Canada and are regular nonbreeding residents in the ASC Region. Various species that occur only marginally or casually were excluded from the analyses.

The neotropical migratory species were chosen as our target group for a number of reasons. A major one is the widespread but erroneous belief that South America is not especially important for neotropical migratory birds. A possible explanation for this misconception is that few ecoregion-based studies have been done of the neotropical migrants that occur in the Andean/Southern Cone Region. The present project seeks to fill this gap. The first objective of the study is to determine the distribution and conservation status of neotropical migrants in all ecoregions and nations of the ASC Region.

Another reason for focusing on neotropical migrants is the close relationship between landscape changes and the survival of migratory birds. The presence of neotropical migrants is strongly associated with numerous bird species endemic to and resident in South America. Preservation of migrants has been identified therefore as an important approach for protecting ecological integrity.

In addition to symbolizing the conservation of ecosystems, migratory birds because of their mobility can serve as a symbol linking the Americas. The neotropical migrants can play a synergistic role in enhancing national and international conservation efforts. Successful conservation of birds now requires these regional and even hemispheric approaches.

The second objective of this study is to encourage hemispheric partnerships through participation in the Conservancy's Migratory Bird Initiative. The initiative seeks to preserve migratory birds by protecting critical habitats throughout the Americas. With birds as an overarching conservation theme, the initiative's goal is a comprehensive program of information gathering and planning leading to a focused strategy of site protection and management. The success of protection efforts in North American breeding grounds is tied to conservation efforts in critical nonbreeding grounds in South America. The hope is that this study will enhance local initiatives, both in the United States and South America, by linking U.S. and Latin American conservation efforts.

Some years ago, The Nature Conservancy, knowing that habitat protection is the heart of any solid conservation agenda, began implementing a program called "Parks in Peril" to enhance existing preservation efforts in Latin America and the Caribbean. The Parks in Peril program, funded by the U.S. Agency for International Development, focuses on helping conservation efforts in a highly important set of protected areas that harbor many key habitats and species of migratory and resident birds.

It is within this rich landscape of Parks in Peril sites and other protected areas that this study analyzed the occurrence and status of neotropical migratory birds. The approach here has been to assess neotropical migrants over entire ecoregions as part of an attempt to develop regional and national conservation strategies in South America.

The present study did not attempt to set priorities for conservation. Determining which regions or parks are most important for preservation will be possible only after up-to-date information on bird population numbers becomes available. The present study is a preliminary effort that is expected to serve as a springboard for future projects that will look at this question of abundance.

In the meantime, this publication can serve as a source of information for the Conservancy's partners, on-the-ground park managers, fundraisers, donors, and other organizations such as Partners in Flight, a coalition of groups interested in bird conservation. The study can provide the information needed by organizations and donors to expand their activities into South America. It is our hope that the appropriate people will conduct on-the-ground verification, update abundance information, and assist with integrating data on neotropical migratory bird distributions with information on other biodiversity elements as the basis for comprehensive conservation actions.

Conservation cannot await the conclusions of science. Rightly, conservationists have begun with what we know today. As we learn more through studies such as the present one, we can target our work more and more effectively.

Lesser yellowlegs and stilt sandpipers wading in the shallow waters of a pond in the Paraguayan chaco, eastern kingbirds descending on a fruiting tree in the yungas of Bolivia, upland sandpipers winging over the paramos of Ecuador, eastern wood-pewees and yellow-billed cuckoos pausing briefly to refuel in the salt-dried scrub of coastal Venezuela, Blackburnian warblers foraging with mixed tanager flocks in the Andean forests of Colombia, sanderlings chasing the waves on the beaches of Peru: these are some of the images of neotropical migrants that spring to mind, and there are a multitude more. We don't want to lose them, and we don't want to see them diminished.

# Chapter 1

# *Approach*

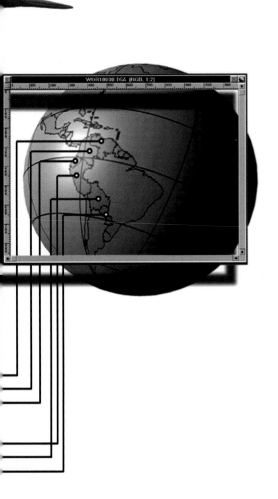

The Migratory Bird Initiative, which was initiated by The Nature Conservancy to pursue its conservation mission, seeks to preserve declining and imperiled migratory bird populations by protecting their most critical habitats throughout the Americas. To help achieve this goal, the Conservancy's Latin America and Caribbean Division initiated a series of studies of migratory birds. The present study is the first in the series and was conducted by the division's Andean/Southern Cone (ASC) Region. It focuses on the nations, ecoregions, and Parks in Peril sites of the ASC Region.

The ASC migratory bird project was an immense task, requiring the compilation, organization, and manipulation of a tremendous amount of data, as well as extensive communication with numerous Latin American partner organizations and experts. To put the results in context, it will help to describe the steps undertaken for this ambitious study. Before looking at the study's methodology, however, we need to define the term *ecoregion* and explore its significance to conservation.

## Ecoregions

The classification of geographical areas into ecoregions has been proposed by a number of scientists.[2] Most agree that ecosystems occur in an orderly hierarchy culminating in ecoregions at the broadest geographical scales. These large-scale ecoregions are appropriate for addressing the conservation of migrants because of the birds' mobility and for other reasons explored below.

The ecoregion system used in the present study was developed by the staff of the World Bank's Environment Unit for Latin America and the Caribbean and the World Wildlife Fund's Conservation Science Program. The World Bank and World Wildlife Fund proposed the system to address the absence of a widely accepted land classification scheme.[3] Their ecoregion scheme represents a powerful land classification system that can be applied to Latin America and the Caribbean.

The World Bank-World Wildlife Fund system emphasizes the consideration of ecological processes in addition to an area's visible biological and physical elements. Specifically, to paraphrase somewhat, an ecoregion is defined as a geographically distinct assemblage of natural communities that *historically* share a large majority of their species, exhibit similar ecological dynamics and environmental conditions, and depend for their long-term persistence on critical ecological interactions.[4]

An ecoregion may contain a variety of habitat types and still be considered a single unit.[5] Ecoregions can vary widely in size. Moreover, individual instances of a given type of ecoregion need not be contiguous. Because of differences in climate, soils, historical processes, or landforms such as mountain ranges, large rivers, or other water bodies, variant kinds of ecosystems can be interspersed within a given ecoregion. To flesh out this discussion, see the glossary at the end of this document for descriptions of ecoregions typical of the ASC Region.

Ecoregions are appropriate units for conservation because they are based on relationships and processes that include living and non-living components of habitats. Conservation planning that takes into account an ecoregional perspective is more likely to preserve these ecological processes and associated components of the landscape. By doing so, the long-run adaptability and sustainability of conserved areas are better maintained, as are functions of the land area that are important to local residents. Ecoregions are thus superior to units based on artificial or crude demarcations such as political boundaries or simple landforms such as a river.

The World Bank-World Wildlife Fund ecoregion system was developed in such a way that the units reflect the minimum level of resolution required for achieving regional representation and effective conservation planning. That is, each ecoregion boundary is intended to identify an area for which a single conservation strategy can be applied effectively.

At the same time, ecoregions can be broken down into smaller portions for focused conservation efforts. Our assessment of neotropical migratory birds in the ASC Region is the first time that the World Bank-World Wildlife Fund ecoregion scheme has been integrated into a conservation endeavor for a specific group of species.

Traditionally, The Nature Conservancy has focused conservation efforts on land and water *habitats* rather than on assemblages of species. There are certain characteristics of

**1**

Approach

birds, migratory birds in particular, that make them as a group an effective flagship for broader conservation endeavors based on ecoregions.

Most neotropical migratory birds are dependent on a number of separate and distinct habitats scattered over two or more nations. Focusing conservation endeavors on these birds therefore directs resources beyond U.S. borders to a wider range of geographic areas, including Latin America and the Caribbean. The ability to link diverse landscapes using a common element such as migratory birds allows for unique partnerships and opportunities for habitat conservation.

Birdwatching is enjoyed by tens of millions of people. Many amateur birders, as well as scientists, value neotropical migratory birds in particular because of the annual nature of their visits and their migratory feats.[6] Studies have shown that humans—both children and adults—prefer beautiful and charming animals over ecologically important, yet less attractive, species.[7] Birds and mammals, because of this appeal, can garner significant political and financial support for efforts to protect habitat.

Avian migrants in particular use a range of habitats that harbor year-round resident and endemic species of birds and other animals. For many reasons, then, neotropical migratory birds can act as effective intercontinental ambassadors to enhance national and international protection of natural habitats.

## Migratory Species and Their Status

The first step in the methodology employed in this study was to identify neotropical migratory birds that frequent the ASC Region. For the purposes of the study, neotropical migrants are defined as those avian species that breed in the United States and Canada and have been recorded during the nonbreeding season in habitats located in South America, Central America, Mexico, and the Caribbean.[8]

We generated initial bird lists for each of the six relevant nations (Bolivia, Colombia, Ecuador, Paraguay, Peru, and Venezuela) using the Conservancy's Biological and Conservation Data System. This vast and comprehensive database is used to manage information related to the ecology, conservation status, management, protection, occurrence, and monitoring of animal and plant species of the western hemisphere.

Based on a review of the literature and the advice of consultants, we expanded the initial lists for each nation into a master list of neotropical migrants. (See Chapter 2.) This list encompasses all the birds that migrate from North America and occur as regular nonbreeders in the ASC Region during the northern winter. It should be noted that some of the migratory species included on the list also have breeding populations in South America. The master list does not include species that occur purely as accidentals or vagrants, that is, species that occur irregularly and in very small numbers.

Once the master list was complete, we broke it down into a comprehensive list for each of the six nations included in the ASC Region. Ecoregions were used next as a sort of "map" to plot bird occurrences in the Parks in Peril sites in each country. Thus, the study's ecoregional approach involved compiling layers of information.

After we developed the national and ecoregion lists, we gathered information on the status of the migratory populations. A number of surveys for monitoring avian populations are available, but most are based on a census of birds on their breeding grounds. The majority of the surveys have limited use for evaluating the conservation status of neotropical migrants as a group. One reason is that the surveys are limited in the number of species covered. In addition, many were conducted at the wrong time of year, have narrow geographic coverage, or fail to provide long-term data.

For this project, we identified two main sources for evaluating conservation status. The first is the North American Breeding Bird Survey, which has been coordinated and maintained since 1966 by the U.S. Fish and Wildlife Service and the Canadian Wildlife Service. The purpose of the survey is to improve understanding of breeding bird abundances and distributions. The agencies have established 3,400 survey routes, each of which is 24.5 miles long with 50 point counts spaced one-half mile apart. The routes are covered once a year (in June in most U.S. states) by dedicated volunteer observers who count all birds sighted or heard calling within a quarter-mile radius of the survey route. The data are submitted to the U.S. Fish and Wildlife Service and subsequently evaluated to produce a series

© Richard Dewey

*At present, bird-banding information on neotropical migratory birds is unavailable for many ecosystems in Latin America and the Caribbean. The ecoregional approach employed in the present study is expected to make it easier to identify long-term monitoring projects such as bird-banding studies, which often rely on volunteers.*

of continental, regional, national, and state population trends.

For the present study, we relied on U.S. long-term population trends for 1966 to 1991, presented as percent decline per year.[9] The number of declining species recorded by the North American Breeding Bird Survey has been subject to recent debate and analysis.[10] Notwithstanding the survey's limitations, we believe that for conservation purposes it is the best available long-term quantitative indicator of bird population trends.

The second main source for determining conservation status is based on figures developed by Partners in Flight for its system of conservation prioritization. Partners in Flight is a coalition of agencies, organizations, and individuals interested in migratory birds and their habitats. The coalition was set up by the National Fish and Wildlife Foundation in 1990.

Partners in Flight encourages national and international partnerships that protect neotropical migratory birds before they become endangered or threatened. Efforts by the groups that make up Partners in Flight include the development of a prioritization scheme that "identifies those birds at any locality on several geographic scales most in need of conservation action."[11] The scheme is based on scores that reflect a species' potential to be extirpated. Scores range from 7 to 30, and species with scores higher than 18 are considered to be of high conservation concern.[12] Unlike the North American Breeding Bird Survey data, which are limited to population trends in North America, the Partners in Flight scores take into account factors from both breeding and nonbreeding grounds.

To assess the status of neotropical migrants, it is necessary to understand the importance of South American destinations to these species. In other words, for which migrants is a habitat in South America the most important destination as opposed to somewhere in Mexico, Central America, or the Caribbean? Answering this question is critical to setting conservation priorities for the group of migrants that have this "South American affinity." They are the species that truly need South American habitats in order to survive. A major outcome of this project is a comprehensive list of neotropical migratory birds with a specific South American affinity.[13]

Finally, as part of our data collection, we clarified the migrants' basic habitat preferences in the ASC Region with respect to aquatic features and disturbed habitats. Within any ecoregion the patterns of distribution and abundance of neotropical migrants (as well as birds in general) are profoundly affected by local habitat features such as the presence of bodies of water and alterations in the native ecosystem wrought by human occupation. Some migrant species are found only in the vicinity of standing water. Others may selectively gravitate toward or shun secondary habitats.

Understanding how birds use available habitats is crucial to assessing the ramifications of habitat threats on species survival. Data on migrant use of various kinds of aquatic and disturbed habitats were collected for each species and nation. Sources used by the study included published reports and correspondence with Conservancy partners, ornithologists, and consultants. Adequate information was unavailable, however, for differentiating between preferences shown by birds as transients during migration versus birds as winter residents.[14]

## Migrants in Ecoregions, Nations, and Parks in Peril

The study described in this document called for ascertaining the migratory bird species of each nation in the ASC Region. It also called for determining the species in more refined geographic areas, specifically ecoregions and Parks in Peril sites.[15] The Parks in Peril program was designed by The Nature Conservancy, together with the Conservancy's Latin American and Caribbean partner organizations, as an emergency effort to safeguard the most important and imperiled natural areas in the hemisphere. The purpose is to ensure an initial level of critical management for each of the targeted protected areas.

The Parks in Peril program is based on building a collaborative partnership among national, international, public, and private organizations. Currently, the program includes a total of 61 sites encompassing more than 74 million acres. Thirty-nine organizations participate in Parks in Peril activities in 18 countries. The U.S. Agency for International Development played a major role in launching and supporting this successful program.

For the present study, the occurrence of species for ecoregions and Partners in Peril sites was determined in a systematic and integrated fashion. Occurrence in each ecoregion was based on habitat descriptions from the literature, species range maps, and additional information provided by consultants.[16] For the Parks in Peril sites, we developed and sent preliminary species lists to the Conservancy's partners and ornithological experts, who confirmed or negated records of birds in the various sites.[17] If a bird species was recorded as occurring within a Parks in Peril site, we assumed that the species was present in the ecoregion or ecoregions that overlap the park's boundaries. Ultimately we generated two types of species lists, one indicating recorded occurrences and the other estimated occurrences.

## Information Management

The needs for information management in this project were considerable, due to the variety of information gathered for each species, ecoregion, Parks in Peril site, and nation. The information was generated from a number of computerized and manual sources and was subsequently recombined in spreadsheets for tabular data analysis and in a geographic information system for mapping purposes.

The Nature Conservancy's new Migratory Bird Information System was used to manage the data. This comprehensive and versatile Microsoft Access® database allows for specific data queries involving all of the geographic, occurrence, and status information. For our geographic information system, we took advantage of leading-edge PC ARC/INFO® and PC ARC/VIEW® software programs, which were invaluable to the spatial analysis and presentation of the study's results.

The analyses performed with the data aim to provide a descriptive, first-cut quantitative assessment of the species richness, distribution, and general conservation status of neotropical migratory bird species in the ASC Region. We believe that this study can serve as the foundation for further projects and for the development of priorities and strategies for migratory bird conservation in other regions.

# Chapter 2

# Regional Assessment

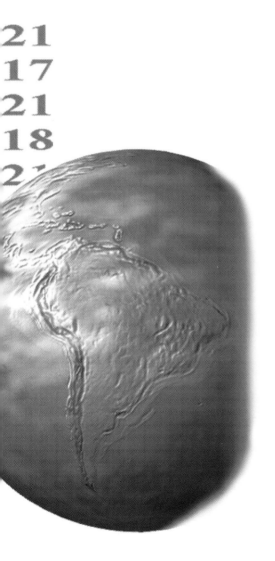

The marvels and mysteries of South America's rich biological diversity have long captured the interest of scientists. The exuberance of life found in the continent's forests and coasts captivates conservation groups and the public as well. The birdlife by itself is enough to account for the increased attention that has occurred in recent decades. Tropical and subtropical ecosystems of South America harbor almost a third (approximately 3,100 species) of all known species of birds on earth.[18]

South America alone contains the highest diversity of endemic birds in the western hemisphere. Endemic birds—native species that occur only in one area of the world—coexist with numerous other resident birds and hundreds of migrants from North America, southern South America, and the Caribbean, as well as a few transoceanic migrants from the Old World. South America's vast territory and amazing wealth of habitats are partly responsible for this proliferation of species. Other contributing factors are the continent's multiple geographic barriers: the Andes and large rivers such as the Amazon and the Orinoco. The fact that the uplifting of the Andes is relatively recent as a geological event also has accelerated the process. As a result, the multiplying of fauna in South America is the most spectacular speciation process that has occurred in the Americas.

## Migratory Birds in South America

Approximately six billion birds migrate between the neotropics and North America every year.[19] Of the 650 species reported as nesting in the United States, the study's research reveals that 62 percent (406 species) have been recorded in Latin America and the Caribbean as nonbreeders.

Of these neotropical migrants, nearly a third (132 species) occur regularly in the Andean/Southern Cone (ASC) Region during the nonbreeding season. Represented in these 132 species are 19 taxonomic families that include landbirds, waterfowl, seabirds, and shorebirds. Also represented are regular transients that pass through the ASC Region on their way to other nonbreeding grounds in South America. (See Table 2.1.)

Despite emerging information on avian diversity in South America, most efforts to protect the nonbreeding grounds of neotropical migrants focus on Mexico, Central America, and selected Caribbean islands. Part of the reason may be the notion that South America is less critical to the survival of these birds than are areas in the rest of Latin America and the Caribbean.

It is true that more species of neotropical migrants winter in those areas. Yet, for many species, habitats in South America are the most important destination. Those species are "programmed" to go to specific geographic destinations—habitats in the 77 ecoregions of the ASC Region. (See Table 2.2 and Figure 2.1.) The habitats these species use, either as transients or nonbreeding residents, include tropical moist forests, dry forests, yungas, paramo, chaco, and coastal and mangrove habitats.

Why do some birds migrate between North and South America? The answer provides a perspective that may enhance the conservation of migratory birds.

Scientists have proposed a number of theories on the evolution of bird migration, but a recent hypothesis suggested by John Rappole combines some elements of previous ideas and seems to best explain the migration of most neotropical migrants. Rappole proposes that most of these species were originally neotropical residents that were forced away from their birthplace by competition with members of their own species. They retreated to the northern temperate zone but were pushed back to the neotropics by deteriorating weather as the northern winter approached.[20]

These species spend only one-third to one-half of their lives on their breeding grounds in North America. This suggests that the traditional North American view of neotropical migrants as "our" birds that are temporary "guests" in the neotropics where they "winter" should be adjusted. To modify this North American bias, certain changes in semantics are needed. For example, the term *nonbreeding grounds* should replace *wintering grounds,* and *nonbreeding resident* should substitute for *winter resident.* Such adjustments might help galvanize conservationists in North America to unite with partners in Latin America to do what is necessary to conserve these birds.

Avian migration from North America to the neotropics is but one of several kinds of migration patterns that take place in the southern part of our hemisphere. Less studied but apparently quite prevalent is the subtropical to neotropical pattern, the migration of birds from Mexico and the West Indies to southern latitudes. Another is the migration of birds within the neotropics. This intratropical migration includes altitudinal migration. Still another is the migration of birds from southern South America toward Amazonia, which is known as austral migration and takes place during the southern hemisphere's winter.

Austral migration and migration from the northern hemisphere constitute the two most conspicuous long-range movements of birds in the neotropics. In terms of the sheer number of species involved, austral migration is more significant than neotropical migration. Arguably, conservation of austral species may be therefore more important for the preservation of biodiversity. A preliminary list of 313 austral migrants is included as an appendix of the present study. Austral migration should be the focus of a follow-up project.

The reason for the focus of the present study, however, is the urgent need to protect habitats that are important to neotropical migrants. Austral migrants generally breed in more open or scrubby habitats than are used by neotropical birds. The australs also choose similarly open areas during the nonbreeding season. This difference in habitat requirements means that a conservation plan that takes into account the needs of neotropical migrants may very well miss important nonbreeding habitats for austral migrants. It underscores the importance of integrating many kinds of data into the prioritization of areas for conservation.

## Distributions in Ecoregions

Given the tremendous variety of ecosystems in the ASC Region, the determination of species distributions of neotropical migrants is a complex undertaking. The task involves establishing the species of neotropical migrants that occur in each of the 77 ecoregions found in the six nations of the ASC Region.

Comparison of species richness across ecoregions and nations must be done with great caution. Major variations in habitat within a given ecoregion are caused by differences in soils, elevation, human disturbance, and hydrographic features, and these variations affect the distribution of birds. The occurrence and abundance of a given neotropical migrant species is therefore not uniform across an ecoregion.

The fact that one ecoregion has more migratory bird species (i.e., a higher species richness) than another does not mean that it is more important for migratory birds. Factors such as the abundance of each species and the status of the birds need to be known before solid conservation priorities can be set.

Identification of the ecoregion distribution of the 132 species in the ASC Region during the nonbreeding season reveals that the greatest number of species occurs along the coastline. (See Figure 2.2.) The ecoregions determined to have the highest species richness are, in descending order, the Cordillera de la Costa forests in Venezuela; the Chocó/Darién moist forests in Colombia, Panama, and Ecuador; the Ecuadorian dry forests; the Guajira/Barranquilla xeric scrub of Colombia and Venezuela; and the La Costa xeric shrublands of Venezuela. (See Table 2.3.) Each of these ecoregions hosts between 65 and 58 species.

The Sinú Valley dry forests in Colombia and the interior Napo moist forests, which extend from Peru through Ecuador and Colombia and a small portion of Venezuela, also are particularly rich in neotropical migratory bird species, hosting 57 species each. Overall, we found a total of 30 ecoregions in the ASC Region that each harbor more than 30 neotropical migratory bird species.

The fact that relatively high numbers of migratory species occur in the coastal ecoregions is not surprising, because shorebirds and seabirds constitute more than one-third of the 132 migrant species that occur in the ASC Region. The high number of migratory species determined to live along the Ecuadorian and Peruvian coasts may be explained by an important natural phenomenon, the Humboldt Current, that affects these coasts. The Humboldt Current is a shallow, cold-water current flowing northwards along the western coast of South America.[21] It causes an upwelling of nutrient-rich waters. The high nutrient levels in turn increase fish and plankton populations, providing migrant birds with a rich oceanic feast. Upwelling is generally most intense along the coast of Peru.[22]

Shorebirds and seabirds have entirely different habitat requirements from landbirds and waterfowl. Exclusion of these species could be expected to affect our study's ecoregional analysis. To determine the impact, we examined the ecoregional occurrence of the subset of neotropical migratory birds comprising landbirds and waterfowl only, excluding from consideration the storm-petrels, plovers, sandpipers, turnstones, surfbirds, phalaropes, gulls, and terns.

The result? We found that among the ecoregions with the highest number of species, several that border the coast are still in the top 10. Included are the Chocó/Darién moist forests, Cordillera de la Costa forests, and Magdalena/Urabá moist forests. However, a few landlocked ecoregions now show some of the highest numbers of species. Among these are ecoregions situated near the upper Andean region, interior Napo moist forests ecoregion, and the Sinú Valley dry forests. The number of species of landbird and waterfowl neotropical migratory birds in the 10 top-ranking ecoregions ranges from 48 to 39.

Neotropical migrants use numerous protected areas in South America as stopover sites or nonbreeding grounds. An important aspect of our analysis was to determine to what extent these species occur in the Parks in Peril sites in the ASC Region. The region has 22 of these sites at present and three protected areas that may be designated as Parks in Peril sites. Altogether, the 25 sites total more than 42 million acres. (See the list in Table 2.4.)

The Parks in Peril sites preserve original habitat for 36 ecoregions and, as a group, provide refuge for at least 101 of the 132 species of migrants to the ASC Region. (See Table 3.1 in Chapter 3.) An additional 28 species are estimated to frequent one or more of these sites but have not yet been recorded. Only the black storm-petrel, Wilson's plover, and the black swift are not listed (i.e., neither recorded nor estimated) for any Parks in Peril site in the ASC Region. The total number of migrants at each site (including recorded and estimated) ranges from 23 to 93 species. The study's findings regarding migratory birds at Parks in Peril sites are discussed further in Chapter 3 in the context of individual nations.

## Migrants with a South American Affinity

Of the 132 species in the ASC Region during the nonbreeding season, our results show that South America is the main or core wintering ground for 53 species. These 53 species, representing 40 percent of the migratory species that occur in the ASC region, are thus neotropical migratory birds with a South American affinity. (See Table 2.1.)

These birds are "perpetual summer-seekers" who presumably benefit from their long-distance migration by maximizing reproduction during the lush northern summer and minimizing mortality during the harsh northern winter. The fact that the majority of the populations of each of these 53 species spends the nonbreeding season in South America indicates that ASC Region habitats and Parks in Peril sites are critical to the protection of these birds.

Our geographical analysis also indicated that the highest numbers of neotropical migrants with a South American affinity occur in two major areas in the interior of the ASC Region. (See Table 2.3 and Figure 2.3.) One area includes the Napo moist forests (39 species) and the eastern Cordillera Real montane forests of Ecuador, Colombia, and Peru (33 species). The second area comprises the southwestern Amazonian moist forests (31 species). The relationship between these findings and current understanding of overall avian species richness is discussed in the next section.

High distribution of species with a South American affinity also is apparent in coastal ecoregions, including the Chocó/Darién moist forests, Cordillera de la Costa forests, Ecuadorian dry forests, and Catatumbo moist forests of Venezuela and Colombia, each of which hosts from 25 to 28 species. A recent study by Robinson et al. confirms this pattern of species richness.[23] Additional ecoregions with high numbers of migrants with a South American affinity are the Bolivian yungas and Chaco savannas of Paraguay and Bolivia.

As with the neotropical migrants in general, we did another evaluation of distribution by excluding shorebirds and seabirds. When this subset was excluded, we found that many of the ecoregions with the greatest species richness overall are also richest in the 53 species with a South American affinity. These ecoregions are the Napo moist forests, eastern Cordillera Real montane forests, Chocó/Darién, and the southwestern Amazonian moist forests. Some interior ecoregions, such as the Cordillera Oriental montane forests and Magdalena/Urabá moist forests, also are among the top 10 ecoregions with respect to species richness of landbirds and waterfowl with a South American affinity.

## Species of Conservation Concern

Which migrant species are most at risk? For the purposes of this study, we singled out a group of migratory species with "conservation concern," based on Partners in Flight (PIF) scores and North American Breeding Bird Survey (BBS) population trends. Included in this group are all species that exhibit one or both of the following: high PIF scores (greater than 18) and statistically significant long-term BBS trends. The species of conservation concern together with their respective PIF prioritization scores and BBS population trends over 25 years are presented in Table 2.1.

The results of our evaluation of conservation status are summarized below:

|  | Total Species | Conservation Concern |
|---|---|---|
| U.S. Neotrop. Migrants | 406 | 156 |
| Migrants to ASC Region | 132 | 48 |
| South America Affinity | 53 | 29 |

By these criteria, an alarming 29 species (55 percent) of the migrants with a South American affinity are of conservation concern. Additional migratory species would join this group if we consider information from other studies.[24] The additional species are the broad-winged hawk, Swainson's hawk, upland sandpiper, barn swallow, American golden-plover, and yellow-green vireo. The addition of these six species makes a grand total of 35 migratory species with a South American affinity that are of conservation concern. This conclusion suggests that *two-thirds of the 53 species with a South American affinity have a tenuous future unless their status can be improved.*

Which ecoregions are utilized by the greatest number of neotropical migratory birds of conservation concern? A tally of species for each ecoregion (see Table 2.3 and Figure 2.4) points to, in descending order, the Cordillera de la Costa forests (28 species), Chocó/Darién moist forests, Napo moist forests, and Catatumbo moist forests (22 species). Of these species of conservation concern, the group with a South American affinity is of particular interest to this study because the future of these birds depends heavily on the fate of their nonbreeding grounds in the ASC Region. (See Table 2.5.) For this group, the same ecoregions are in the top five with respect to species richness except for the Catatumbo moist forests, which are replaced by the eastern Cordillera Real montane forests. The number of species per ecoregion in this analysis ranges from 20 (Napo moist forests) to 15 (Venezuelan islands).

## Refugia and Endemic Centers

Focusing on the migrants that hail from the north runs the risk of losing overall perspective on neotropical bird conservation. An appealing yet controversial theory on speciation postulated by Jurgen Haffer[25] sparks an intriguing question of whether a cause-and-effect relationship

might exist between the distributions of migrants in the ancient and current forests of the ASC Region.

Haffer's theory is based on the assumption that climatic fluctuations in the last million years or so (Pleistocene period) resulted in the expansion of arid habitats at the expense of humid forests. The patches of humid forest that survived served as refuges or "refugia" for forest animals. After thousands of years of isolation, new Amazonian species evolved from the parent populations inhabiting these refugia. Haffer proposed 16 such forest refugia in Central and South America, seven of which occur within the ASC Region. Haffer's selection of probable refugia was based on current distribution patterns of birds, and these refugia are currently considered among the most species-rich places on Earth.

We overlapped Haffer's postulated forest refugia with the corresponding ecoregion (or, in some cases, ecoregions). We then overlapped the number of migratory species, excluding shorebirds and seabirds because these are not forest-dependent species. Interestingly, our results show that the ecoregions most rich in landbirds and waterfowl overlap with all of Haffer's refugia, with the exception of the Tepuis refugia. It is conceivable that the locations of the ancient forest refugia are ingrained in some neotropical migrants through learned or inherited migratory tendencies passed down through generations of birds.

These species-rich refugia are also home to many endemic species. Endemics by definition rely on distinct and limited geographic areas and are particularly vulnerable to habitat loss and other threats. We examined the relationship between the distribution patterns for neotropical migrants and endemic birds using data on areas with high avian endemism, known as Endemic

Bird Areas, as developed by Birdlife International.[26]

Endemic Bird Areas serve as strategic conservation "red flags" by marking places where global extinctions would be caused by the destruction or modification of the habitat. Using Endemic Bird Area maps, we estimated the number of these areas that occur within each ecoregion. (See Table 2.2.) In examining these areas, we discovered that they are often concentrated in the locations of the seven ASC Region refugia identified by Haffer. A correspondence between Haffer's refugia and centers of endemism also was noted by Ridgely.[27]

Ecoregions that have high numbers of migratory species and contain four Endemic Bird Areas include the northwestern Andean montane forests and the eastern Cordillera Real montane forests. These same ecoregions, along with the Peruvian yungas, also constitute the group with the highest number of species of conservation concern. In these ecoregions, the study found a low number of species with a South American affinity, with the exception of the eastern Cordillera Real montane forests.

These results have been supported elsewhere. Ridgely and Tudor (1989) note: "The high rainfall zone where the Amazonian forests meet the Andean foothills has the highest avian diversity of any region of the world."[28] According to Birdlife International, half of the Amazonian Endemic Bird Areas are in this region, and there are several more in the lower parts of the adjacent foothills.[29]

Most of the species with a South American affinity are found in ecoregions with low endemism. Overall, high numbers of migratory species occur in places that are home to a high number of resident bird species, including endemics. The relationship between endemic species and migratory species needs additional research in many areas of South America. Endemic Bird Areas are indeed critical for developing conservation priorities in the region.

Birdlife International has classified some Endemic Bird Areas as particularly important because of the threatened status of the range-restricted birds inhabiting them. Among the most striking examples are the East Andes of Colombia, subtropical inter-Andean Colombia, Chocó and Pacific-slope Andes, Tumbesian western Ecuador and Peru, and the high Peruvian Andes, each home to more than 10 threatened species.[30] There are 11 ecoregions with high migrant species richness as well as one or two threatened Endemic Bird Areas in the Andes and to the west. (See Tables 2.2 and 2.3 and Figure 2.2.)[31]

## Table 2.1 Neotropical Migratory Birds of the Andean/Southern Cone Region: Conservation Status and Sensitivity to Habitat Alteration

Characteristics of migrants, including South American Affinity, conservation concern (as indicated by high Partners in Flight concern scores and/or US Breeding Bird Survey population declines), and traits indicating sensitivity to habitat alteration are presented. See footnotes for details.

| Family | Scientific Name | Common Name | S. Amer. Affinity [2] | Concern [3] | PIF > 18 [4] | Decline [5] | Level of Sig. [6] | Habitat Spec. | Pref. 1o Habitat | Site Fidelity | Vul. Trop. Defor. [1] |
|---|---|---|---|---|---|---|---|---|---|---|---|
| **HYDROBATIDAE** (Storm-Petrels) | Oceanodroma leucorhoa | Leach's storm-petrel | | ● | | nt | | | | | |
| | Oceanodroma melania | black storm-petrel | | ● | 22 | nt | | | | | |
| | Oceanodroma microsoma | least storm-petrel | | | 24 | nt | | | | | |
| **ARDEIDAE** (Bitterns and Herons) | Ixobrychus exilis | least bittern | + | | | | | | | | |
| | Ardea herodias | great blue heron | | | | | | | Y | | |
| | Casmerodius albus | great egret | + | | | | | | | | |
| | Egretta thula | snowy egret | + | | | | | | | | |
| | Egretta caerulea | little blue heron | + | | | -1.2 | | | | | |
| | Bubulcus ibis | cattle egret | + | | | | | | | | |
| | Butorides virescens | green heron | + | | | nt | | | Y | | |
| **ANATIDAE** (Ducks) | Anas acuta | northern pintail | | | | -32.9 | | | Y | | |
| | Anas discors | blue-winged teal | | | | -3.5 | | | Y | Y | |
| | Anas cyanoptera | cinnamon teal | | | | | | | Y | | |

Table 2. (continued)

| Family (Order) | Scientific name | Common name | | | | Trend | | |
|---|---|---|---|---|---|---|---|---|
| **ANATIDAE** (Ducks) (continued) | *Anas clypeata* | northern shoveler | | | | -0.6 | Y | |
| | *Anas americana* | American wigeon | | | | | Y | |
| | *Aythya affinis* | lesser scaup | | | | | Y | |
| **CATHARTIDAE** (Vultures) | + *Cathartes aura* | turkey vulture | | | | | | |
| **ACCIPITRIDAE** (Kites, Hawks and Ospreys) | + *Pandion haliaetus* | osprey | ● | ● | nt | | Y | |
| | *Elanoides forficatus* | American swallow-tailed kite | ● | ● | 24 | | Y | |
| | *Ictinia mississippiensis* | Mississippi kite | ● | | 19 | | | |
| | *Buteo platypterus* | broad-winged hawk | ● | | | | Y | |
| | *Buteo swainsoni* | Swainson's hawk | | | | | Y | Y |
| **FALCONIDAE** (Falcons) | *Falco columbarius* | merlin | | | | -0.1 | | |
| | + *Falco peregrinus* | peregrine falcon | | | | | | |
| **RALLIDAE** (Rails) | *Porzana carolina* | sora | | | | -9.9 | | |
| **CHARADRIIDAE** (Plovers) | *Pluvialis squatarola* | black-bellied plover | | | | nt | | |
| | *Pluvialis dominica* | American golden-plover | | | | nt | | |
| | *Charadrius wilsonia* | Wilson's plover | ● | ● | 20 | nt | | Y |
| | *Charadrius semipalmatus* | semipalmated plover | | | | | | |
| | *Charadrius vociferus* | killdeer | | | | | | |
| **SCOLOPACIDAE** (Sandpipers, Phalaropes and Allies) | *Tringa melanoleuca* | greater yellowlegs | | | | nt | | |
| | *Tringa flavipes* | lesser yellowlegs | | | | -1.7 | | |
| | *Tringa solitaria* | solitary sandpiper | ● | | | nt | | |
| | *Catoptrophorus semipalmatus* | willet | | | | nt | | |
| | *Heteroscelus incanus* | wandering tattler | | | | -0.4 | | |
| | *Actitis macularia* | spotted sandpiper | | | | | | |
| | *Bartramia longicauda* | upland sandpiper | ● | | | | | Y |

2

Table

35

**Table 2.1** Neotropical Migratory Birds of the Andean/Southern Cone Region: Conservation Status and Sensitivity to Habitat Alteration (continued)

| Family | Scientific Name | Common Name | Conservation Status | | | | | Sensitivity to Habitat Alteration[1] | | | |
| | | | S. Amer. Affinity[2] | Concern[3] | PIF > 18[4] | Decline[5] | Level of Sig.[6] | Habitat Spec. | Pref. 1o Habitat | Site Fidelity | Vul. Trop. Defor. |
|---|---|---|---|---|---|---|---|---|---|---|---|
| SCOLOPACIDAE (Sandpipers, Phalaropes and Allies) (continued) | Numenius phaeopus | whimbrel | ● | | | nt | | | | | |
| | Limosa haematica | Hudsonian godwit | | ● | 22 | nt | | | | | |
| | Arenaria interpres | ruddy turnstone | | ● | | nt | | | | | |
| | Aphriza virgata | surfbird | | | 19 | nt | | | | | |
| | Calidris canutus | red knot | | ● | 22 | nt | | | | Y | |
| | Calidris alba | sanderling | | | | nt | | | | Y | |
| | Calidris pusilla | semipalmated sandpiper | ● | | | nt | | | | | |
| | Calidris mauri | western sandpiper | ● | | | nt | | | | | |
| | Calidris minutilla | least sandpiper | ● | | | nt | | | | | |
| | Calidris fuscicollis | white-rumped sandpiper | ● | ● | 21 | nt | | | | | |
| | Calidris bairdii | Baird's sandpiper | ● | | | nt | | | | | |
| | Calidris melanotos | pectoral sandpiper | ● | | | nt | | | | | |
| | Calidris himantopus | stilt sandpiper | | ● | 20 | nt | | | | | |
| | Tryngites subruficollis | buff-breasted sandpiper | | ● | 22 | nt | | | | Y | |
| | Limnodromus griseus | short-billed dowitcher | | | | nt | | | | Y | |
| + | Gallinago gallinago | common snipe | | | | | | | | | |
| | Steganopus tricolor | Wilson's phalarope | ● | | | -0.8 | | | | | |
| | Phalaropus lobatus | red-necked phalarope | | | | nt | | | | | |
| | Phalaropus fulicaria | red phalarope | ● | | | nt | | | | | |

| Family / Subfamily | Scientific name | Common name | ● | ● | n | Trend | Sig. | | |
|---|---|---|:--:|:--:|---|---|---|:--:|:--:|
| **LARIDAE** (Gulls and Terns) | *Stercorarius pomarinus* | pomarine jaeger | | ● | | nt | | | |
| | *Stercorarius parasiticus* | parasitic jaeger | | | | nt | | | |
| | *Stercorarius longicaudus* | long-tailed jaeger | | | | nt | | | |
| | *Larus atricilla* | laughing gull | | ● | | | | | |
| | *Larus pipixcan* | Franklin's gull | ● | ● | 23 | -19.3 | *** | | |
| | *Xema sabini* | Sabine's gull | | | | nt | | | |
| | *Sterna nilotica* | gull-billed tern | | | | -0.9 | | | |
| | *Sterna maxima* | royal tern | | | | -2.0 | | | |
| | *Sterna elegans* | elegant tern | ● | ● | 19 | nt | | | |
| | *Sterna sandvicensis* | sandwich tern | | | | | | | |
| | *Sterna dougallii* | roseate tern | | | | nt | | | |
| | *Sterna hirundo* | common tern | ● | ● | | -8.4 | *** | | |
| | *Sterna paradisaea* | Arctic tern | | | | nt | | | |
| | *Sterna antillarum* | least tern | ● | ● | 19 | -2.8 | *** | | |
| | *Chlidonias niger* | black tern | ● | ● | | -5.6 | *** | Y | Y |
| **CUCULIDAE** (Cuckoos) | *Coccyzus erythropthalmus* | black-billed cuckoo | ● | ● | 20 | -0.1 | | Y | |
| | *Coccyzus americanus* | yellow-billed cuckoo | ● | ● | 21 | -1.3 | *** | Y | Y |
| **CAPRIMULGIDAE** (Nighthawks) | + *Chordeiles acutipennis* | lesser nighthawk | | | | -0.1 | | | |
| | *Chordeiles minor* | common nighthawk | ● | ● | | -0.9 | | Y | |
| | *Caprimulgus carolinensis* | chuck-will's-widow | | | | | | | |
| **APODIDAE** (Swifts) | *Cypseloides niger* | black swift | ● | | 24 | -3.5 | | Y | |
| | *Chaetura pelagica* | chimney swift | ● | ● | | -0.7 | | | |
| **ALCEDINIDAE** (Kingfishers) | *Megaceryle alcyon* | belted kingfisher | ● | ● | | -0.7 | | Y | |
| **TYRANNIDAE** (Tyrant Flycatchers) | *Contopus borealis* | olive-sided flycatcher | ● | ● | 20 | -3.7 | *** | Y | Y |
| | *Contopus sordidulus* | western wood-pewee | ● | ● | | -1.7 | *** | Y | |
| | *Contopus virens* | eastern wood-pewee | ● | ● | 19 | -1.5 | *** | Y | |
| | *Empidonax virescens* | Acadian flycatcher | ● | ● | 19 | nt | | Y | Y |
| | ++ *Empidonax alnorum* | alder flycatcher | | ● | | nt | | Y | |

Table 2

37

**Table 2.1** Neotropical Migratory Birds of the Andean/Southern Cone Region: Conservation Status and Sensitivity to Habitat Alteration (continued)

| Family | Scientific Name | Common Name | S. Amer. Affinity[2] | Concern[3] | PIF > 18[4] | Decline[5] | Level of Sig.[6] | Habitat Spec. | Pref. 1o Habitat | Site Fidelity | Vul. Trop. Defor. |
|---|---|---|---|---|---|---|---|---|---|---|---|
| | | | | | | | | Conservation Status → ← Sensitivity to Habitat Alteration[1] | | | |
| **TYRANNIDAE** (Tyrant Flycatchers) (continued) | ++ Empidonax traillii | willow flycatcher | • | | nt | nt | | | | Y | |
| | Myiarchus crinitus | great crested flycatcher | • | • | 20 | | | | | | |
| | Myiodynastes luteiventris | sulphur-bellied flycatcher | • | | | -0.3 | | | | | |
| | Tyrannus tyrannus | eastern kingbird | | | 19 | -2.6 | *** | | | | |
| | Tyrannus dominicensis | gray kingbird | | • | | | | | | | |
| **HIRUNDINIDAE** (Swallows) | Progne subis | purple martin | • | | | -0.1 | | | | | |
| | Riparia riparia | bank swallow | • | | | | | | | | |
| | Hirundo pyrrhonota | cliff swallow | • | | | | | | | | |
| | Hirundo rustica | barn swallow | • | | | | | | | | |
| **MUSCICAPIDAE** (Thrushes) | Catharus fuscescens | veery | • | • | 19 | -1.0 | ** | Y | | | |
| | Catharus minimus | gray-cheeked thrush | • | • | | -1.7 | ** | | Y | Y | |
| | Catharus ustulatus | Swainson's thrush | • | | | -0.9 | | N | Y | Y | Y |
| **VIREONIDAE** (Vireos) | Vireo flavifrons | yellow-throated vireo | | • | 19 | | | Y | Y | Y | Y |
| | Vireo olivaceus | red-eyed vireo | • | | | | | | | | |
| | Vireo altiloquus | black-whiskered vireo | • | • | 19 | | | Y | Y | Y | Y |
| | Vireo flavoviridis | yellow-green vireo | • | | | nt | | | | | |

**EMBERIZIDAE**
**(Songbirds and Allies)**

|  |  | | | | | | | | |
|---|---|:--:|:--:|:--:|:--:|:--:|:--:|:--:|:--:|
| *Vermivora chrysoptera* | golden-winged warbler | • | | 25 | -2.6 | *** | Y | Y | |
| *Vermivora peregrina* | Tennessee warbler | | | | | | Y | N | |
| *Dendroica petechia* | yellow warbler | • | | 22 | -0.4 | | Y | Y | Y |
| *Dendroica pensylvanica* | chestnut-sided warbler | | | | | | Y | Y | Y |
| *Dendroica magnolia* | magnolia warbler | | | 19 | | | Y | D | D |
| *Dendroica tigrina* | Cape May warbler | • | | 19 | | | Y | Y | N |
| *Dendroica caerulescens* | black-throated blue warbler | • | | 21 | | | Y | Y | N |
| *Dendroica coronata* | yellow-rumped warbler | | | | | | Y | Y | Y |
| *Dendroica virens* | black-throated green warbler | | • | | | | Y | | |
| *Dendroica fusca* | Blackburnian warbler | • | • | 21 | | | Y | Y | Y |
| *Dendroica castanea* | bay-breasted warbler | • | • | 19 | -1.3 | | Y | | D |
| *Dendroica striata* | blackpoll warbler | • | • | | -8.9 | | Y | Y | Y |
| *Dendroica cerulea* | cerulean warbler | • | | 25 | -2.9 | *** | Y | Y | Y |
| *Mniotilta varia* | black-and-white warbler | • | | | -1.1 | ** | D | D | D |
| *Setophaga ruticilla* | American redstart | • | | | -1.1 | * | D | Y | D |
| *Protonotaria citrea* | prothonotary warbler | • | | 22 | -0.2 | | Y | Y | Y |
| *Seiurus aurocapillus* | ovenbird | | | | | | Y | Y | Y |
| *Seiurus noveboracensis* | northern waterthrush | | | | | | Y | Y | Y |
| *Seiurus motacilla* | Louisiana waterthrush | | | | | | D | Y | D |
| *Oporornis formosus* | Kentucky warbler | • | | 21 | | | | | |
| *Oporornis agilis* | Connecticut warbler | • | • | 21 | -0.7 | | N | N | N |
| *Oporornis philadelphia* | mourning warbler | • | • | 19 | | | Y | Y | |
| *Geothlypis trichas* | common yellowthroat | | | | -0.2 | | Y | Y | Y |
| *Wilsonia citrina* | hooded warbler | • | | 20 | | | Y | Y | |
| *Wilsonia canadensis* | Canada warbler | • | • | 20 | -0.2 | | Y | Y | Y |
| *Piranga rubra* | summer tanager | | | | | | Y | | Y |
| *Piranga olivacea* | scarlet tanager | • | • | 19 | -0.2 | | Y | Y | Y |
| *Pheucticus ludovicianus* | rose-breasted grosbeak | • | • | | | | Y | Y | Y |

Table
2

39

Table 2.1 *Neotropical Migratory Birds of the Andean/Southern Cone Region: Conservation Status and Sensitivity to Habitat Alteration (continued)*

| Family | Scientific Name | Common Name | S. Amer. Affinity[2] | Conservation Status | | | | Sensitivity to Habitat Alteration[1] | | | |
|---|---|---|---|---|---|---|---|---|---|---|---|
| | | | | Concern[3] | PIF >18[4] | Decline[5] | Level of Sig.[6] | Habitat Spec. | Pref. 1° Habitat | Site Fidelity | Vul. Trop. Defor. |
| EMBERIZIDAE (Songbirds and Allies) (continued) | *Spiza americana* | dickcissel | ● | ● | 21 | -1.7 | *** | | | | |
| | *Dolichonyx oryzivorus* | bobolink | ● | ● | | -1.9 | *** | | | | |
| | *Icterus spurius* | orchard oriole | | ● | 20 | -1.4 | ** | N | N | Y | |
| | *Icterus galbula* | northern oriole | | | | | | N | N | Y | |
| | **Totals:** | | 53 | 48 | 43 | 45 | 17 | 14 | 30 | 45 | 13 |

+ Difficulty in distinguishing between ranges of South American residents vs. North American migrants or subspecies.
++ Difficulty in distinguishing between two species of flycatchers.

[1] Information for nonbreeding season in Latin America was compiled from many sources, listed below.
Y = yes, N = no, D = depends; has been categorized both as a specialist and a generalist in different studies. Hab. Specialist = Mostly occurs in one habitat type. Pref. 1° Habitat = Shows a preference for primary habitat. Site Fidelity = Nonbreeding ground site fidelity has been recorded. Vul. Trop. Defor. = Considered highly vulnerable to tropical deforestation. Blanks indicate that specific information was not available.

[2] Neotropical Migratory Bird with a South American Affinity.

[3] Species of conservation concern: Species with PIF concern scores that are >18 and/or statistically significant negative Breeding Bird Survey population trends.

[4] Partners in Flight concern score is greater than 18. nt = no trend available.

[5] Breeding Bird Survey U.S. trend (1966–1991). Statistically significant declines are presented. nt = no trend available. Level of significance is found in next column.

[6] Level of Significance for population trends (*=p<.10; **=p<.05; ***=p<.01).

Sources: Blake and Loiselle 1989; Greenberg 1989; Holmes and Sherry 1989; Hutto 1989; Kricher and Davis 1989; Lynch 1989; Mabey and Morton 1989; Morton 1989; Rappole *et al.* 1989; Rappole 1995; Reed 1989; Robbins *et al.* 1989a; Robbins *et al.* 1989b; Staicer 1989; and David Ewert, personal communication 1995.

## Table 2.2 *Ecoregions of the Andean/Southern Cone Region of South America*

Characteristics of the ecoregions of the region including area, conservation status (ranging from 1 = critical to 5 = relatively intact) and number of Endemic Bird Areas are presented. See footnotes for details.

| Ecoregion [1] | Area (km²) | Cons.[2] Status | EBAs[3] |
|---|---|---|---|
| 1  Amazonian savannas - Colombia, Venezuela | 18,011 | 4 | 0 |
| 2  Andean Yungas - Bolivia | 21,858 | 3 | 2 |
| 3  Araya and Pará xeric scrub - Venezuela | 5,424 | 2 | 2 |
| 4  Beni savannas - Bolivia | 165,403 | 2 | 0 |
| 5  Beni swamp and gallery forests - Bolivia | 15,369 | 4 | 0 |
| 6  Bolivian lowland dry forests - Bolivia | 102,362 | 1 | 0 |
| 7  Bolivian montane dry forests - Bolivia | 39,368 | 1 | 1 |
| 8  Bolivian Yungas - Bolivia | 72,517 | 2 | 2 |
| 9  Brazilian Interior Atlantic forests - Paraguay | 80,299 | 2 | 1 |
| 10 Catatumbo moist forests - Colombia, Venezuela | 21,813 | 1 | 0 |
| 11 Cauca Valley dry forests - Colombia | 5,130 | 1 | 1 |
| 12 Cauca Valley montane forests - Colombia | 32,412 | 1 | 1 |
| 13 Central Andean dry puna - Bolivia, Colombia, Peru | 78,051 | 3 | 0 |
| 14 Central Andean puna - Bolivia, Peru | 140,960 | 3 | 2 |
| 15 Central Andean wet puna - Bolivia, Peru | 184,067 | 3 | 2 |
| 16 Cerrado - Bolivia, Paraguay | 28,387 | 3 | 0 |
| 17 Chaco savannas - Bolivia, Paraguay | 281,378 | 3 | 0 |
| 18 Chocó/Darién moist forests - Colombia, Ecuador | 69,001 | 3 | 1 |
| 19 Cordillera Central paramo - Ecuador, Peru | 14,128 | 3 | 3 |
| 20 Cordillera de Mérida paramo - Venezuela | 3,518 | 4 | 1 |
| 21 Cordillera de La Costa forests - Venezuela | 13,481 | 3 | 2 |
| 22 Cordillera Oriental montane forests - Colombia, Venezuela | 66,712 | 3 | 1 |
| 23 Eastern Cordillera Real montane forest - Colombia, Ecuador, Peru | 84,442 | 3 | 4 |
| 24 Eastern Panamanian montane forests - Colombia | 789 | 3 | 0 |
| 25 Ecuadorian dry forests - Ecuador | 22,271 | 1 | 1 |
| 26 Galapagos Islands xeric scrub- Ecuador | 9,122 | 3 | 1 |
| 27 Guajira/Barranquilla xeric scrub - Colombia, Venezuela | 32,402 | 2 | 1 |
| 28 Guayaquil flooded grasslands - Ecuador | 3,617 | 2 | 1 |
| 29 Guianan highlands moist forests- Colombia, Venezuela | 203,977 | 5 | 1 |
| 30 Guianan moist forests - Venezuela | 31,931 | 3 | 1 |
| 31 Guianan savannas - Venezuela | 13,160 | 4 | 0 |
| 32 Humid Chaco - Bolivia, Paraguay | 152,968 | 3 | 0 |
| 33 Japura/Negro moist forests - Colombia, Peru, Venezuela | 384,906 | 5 | 2 |
| 34 Juruá moist forests - Peru | 36,157 | 5 | 0 |
| 35 La Costa xeric shrublands - Venezuela | 64,379 | 2 | 2 |
| 36 Lara/Falcón dry forests - Venezuela | 16,178 | 2 | 2 |
| 37 Llanos - Colombia, Venezuela | 355,112 | 4 | 1 |
| 38 Llanos dry forests - Venezuela | 44,177 | 2 | 1 |
| 39 Macarena montane forests- Colombia | 2,366 | 3 | 0 |
| 40 Magdalena Valley dry forests - Colombia | 13,837 | 1 | 1 |

| Ecoregion [1] | Area (km$^2$) | Cons.[2] Status | EBAs[3] |
|---|---|---|---|
| 41 Magdalena Valley montane forests - Colombia | 49,322 | 1 | 0 |
| 42 Magdalena/Urabá moist forests - Colombia | 73,660 | 2 | 1 |
| 43 Mangroves* - Colombia | 5,265 | na | 1 |
| 44 Mangroves* - Ecuador | 2,811 | na | 1 |
| 45 Mangroves* - Peru | 701 | na | 1 |
| 46 Mangroves* - Venezuela | 4,595 | na | 0 |
| 47 Maracaibo dry forests - Colombia, Venezuela | 31,471 | 2 | 1 |
| 48 Marañón dry forests - Peru | 14,921 | 2 | 1 |
| 49 Napo moist forests - Colombia, Ecuador, Peru, Venezuela | 369,847 | 4 | 1 |
| 50 Northern Andean paramo - Colombia, Ecuador, Venezuela | 58,806 | 3 | 3 |
| 51 Northwestern Andean montane forests - Colombia, Ecuador | 52,937 | 2 | 4 |
| 52 Orinoco Delta swamp forests- Venezuela | 28,469 | 4 | 0 |
| 53 Orinoco wetlands- Venezuela | 6,403 | 4 | 0 |
| 54 Pantanal - Bolivia, Paraguay | 15,114 | 3 | 0 |
| 55 Paraguaná restingas - Venezuela | 88 | 2 | 1 |
| 56 Paraguaná xeric scrub - Venezuela | 15,313 | 2 | 1 |
| 57 Patia dry forests - Colombia | 1,291 | 1 | 1 |
| 58 Pelagic* - Colombia | na | na | 0 |
| 59 Pelagic* - Ecuador | na | na | 0 |
| 60 Pelagic* - Peru | na | na | 0 |
| 61 Pelagic* - Venezuela | na | na | 0 |
| 62 Peruvian Yungas - Peru | 188,735 | 2 | 4 |
| 63 Rondônia/Mato Grosso moist forests - Bolivia | 70,562 | 3 | 1 |
| 64 Santa Marta montane forests - Colombia | 4,707 | 3 | 1 |
| 65 Santa Marta paramo - Colombia | 1,329 | 3 | 1 |
| 66 Sechura desert - Peru | 188,492 | 3 | 2 |
| 67 Sinú Valley dry forests - Colombia | 55,473 | 1 | 2 |
| 68 Southwestern Amazonia moist forests - Bolivia, Peru | 327,601 | 4 | 1 |
| 69 Tepuis - Venezuela | 46,180 | 5 | 1 |
| 70 Tumbes/Piura dry forests - Ecuador, Peru | 46,341 | 2 | 1 |
| 71 Ucayali moist forests - Peru | 173,527 | 3 | 3 |
| 72 Varzea forests - Colombia, Ecuador, Peru | 58,917 | 3 | 1 |
| 73 Venezuelan Andes montane forests - Colombia, Venezuela | 16,638 | 2 | 1 |
| 74 Venezuelan Islands* - Venezuela | na | na | 0 |
| 75 Western Amazon flooded grasslands - Bolivia, Peru | 10,111 | 4 | 1 |
| 76 Western Amazon swamp forests - Colombia, Peru | 8,315 | 4 | 0 |
| 77 Western Ecuador moist forests - Colombia, Ecuador | 40,218 | 1 | 2 |

[1] Ecoregions derived from the WB/WWF Conservation Assessment (Dinerstein *et al*. 1995). Areas are for ecoregion coverage within nations of the ASC Region only.

* This ecoregion designation was created for this study and does not conform to WB/WWF dataset.

[2] Ecoregional Final Conservation Status ( from Dinerstein *et al*. 1995): 1 = Critical, 2 = Endangered, 3 =Vulnerable, 4 = Relatively Stable, 5 = Relatively Intact.

[3] Endemic Bird Areas (EBA) developed by Birdlife International. EBAs within ASC portion of ecoregions are indicated.

# Table 2.3 Distribution and Conservation Status of Neotropical Migratory Birds in Andean/Southern Cone Nations and Ecoregions

Species richness, number (and percent) of conservation concern (as indicated by high Partners in Flight concern scores and/or U.S. Breeding Bird Survey population declines) for all migrants and for the subset of migrants with a South American Affinity are given. See footnotes for details.

| | All Neotropical Migrants | | | | | Migrants with a South American Affinity | | | | | |
| | Species | Cons. Concern[1] # | % | PIF[2] >18 | BBS Trends[3] # | Dec. | Species | Cons. Concern[1] # | % | PIF[2] >18 | BBS Trends[3] # | Dec. |
|---|---|---|---|---|---|---|---|---|---|---|---|---|
| **Nation** | | | | | | | | | | | | |
| Colombia | 131 | 47 | 35 | 41 | 94 | 16 | 53 | 29 | 54 | 25 | 39 | 12 |
| Venezuela | 111 | 40 | 36 | 33 | 84 | 16 | 45 | 25 | 55 | 21 | 35 | 11 |
| Ecuador | 97 | 32 | 33 | 25 | 61 | 12 | 47 | 23 | 48 | 19 | 33 | 9 |
| Peru | 84 | 29 | 35 | 22 | 51 | 12 | 46 | 23 | 50 | 19 | 32 | 9 |
| Bolivia | 43 | 16 | 37 | 14 | 31 | 8 | 33 | 16 | 48 | 14 | 24 | 8 |
| Paraguay | 28 | 9 | 32 | 8 | 19 | 2 | 22 | 9 | 40 | 8 | 14 | 2 |
| **Ecoregion[4]** | | | | | | | | | | | | |
| Cordillera de La Costa forests - Venezuela | 65 | 28 | 43 | 22 | 54 | 13 | 26 | 17 | 65 | 14 | 21 | 8 |
| Chocó/Darién moist forests - Colombia, Ecuador | 63 | 25 | 40 | 21 | 52 | 11 | 28 | 17 | 60 | 15 | 23 | 8 |
| Ecuadorian dry forests - Ecuador | 63 | 17 | 27 | 14 | 37 | 7 | 25 | 11 | 44 | 10 | 15 | 5 |
| Guajira/Barranquilla xeric scrub - Colombia, Venezuela | 62 | 14 | 23 | 12 | 42 | 6 | 15 | 7 | 46 | 6 | 9 | 4 |
| Venezuelan Islands* - Venezuela | 60 | 24 | 40 | 18 | 53 | 12 | 26 | 15 | 57 | 12 | 25 | 9 |
| La Costa xeric shrublands - Venezuela | 58 | 17 | 29 | 11 | 45 | 8 | 18 | 10 | 55 | 7 | 14 | 5 |
| Napo moist forests - Peru, Ecuador, Colombia, Venezuela | 57 | 24 | 42 | 18 | 44 | 11 | 39 | 20 | 51 | 16 | 30 | 8 |
| Sinú Valley dry forests - Colombia | 57 | 16 | 28 | 14 | 45 | 8 | 16 | 9 | 56 | 8 | 14 | 5 |

Table 2

43

*Table 2.3* Distribution and Conservation Status of Neotropical Migratory Birds in Andean/Southern Cone Nations and Ecoregions (continued)

| Ecoregion[4] | All Neotropical Migrants | | | | | | Migrants with a South American Affinity | | | | | |
|---|---|---|---|---|---|---|---|---|---|---|---|---|
| | Species[4] | Cons. Concern[1] # | % | PIF[2] >18 | BBS Trends[3] # | Dec. | Species[4] | Cons. Concern[1] # | % | PIF[2] >18 | BBS Trends[3] # | Dec. |
| Sechura desert - Peru | 54 | 14 | 26 | 10 | 26 | 5 | 23 | 9 | 39 | 7 | 13 | 3 |
| Cordillera Oriental montane forests - Colombia, Venezuela | 53 | 18 | 34 | 14 | 51 | 9 | 23 | 11 | 47 | 8 | 22 | 6 |
| Eastern Cordillera Real montane forest - Ecuador, Colombia, Peru | 52 | 20 | 38 | 15 | 44 | 10 | 33 | 17 | 51 | 14 | 27 | 7 |
| Northwestern Andean montane forests - Colombia, Ecuador | 49 | 19 | 39 | 16 | 43 | 8 | 24 | 13 | 54 | 12 | 21 | 5 |
| Catatumbo moist forests - Venezuela, Colombia | 48 | 22 | 46 | 19 | 43 | 10 | 25 | 14 | 56 | 12 | 22 | 7 |
| Galapagos Islands xeric scrub- Ecuador | 46 | 8 | 17 | 6 | 24 | 3 | 16 | 5 | 31 | 4 | 10 | 2 |
| Llanos - Venezuela, Colombia | 46 | 11 | 24 | 8 | 35 | 7 | 20 | 8 | 40 | 6 | 15 | 5 |
| Western Ecuador moist forests - Ecuador, Colombia | 45 | 14 | 31 | 11 | 33 | 6 | 16 | 9 | 56 | 8 | 14 | 4 |
| Magdalena/Urabá moist forests - Colombia | 43 | 19 | 44 | 16 | 40 | 7 | 21 | 12 | 57 | 11 | 19 | 4 |
| Southwestern Amazonia moist forests - Peru, Bolivia | 41 | 15 | 37 | 13 | 30 | 6 | 31 | 14 | 45 | 13 | 23 | 5 |
| Venezuelan Andes montane forests - Venezuela, Colombia | 39 | 16 | 41 | 13 | 38 | 7 | 20 | 11 | 55 | 9 | 20 | 5 |
| Cauca Valley montane forests - Colombia | 38 | 18 | 47 | 15 | 36 | 7 | 19 | 11 | 57 | 10 | 17 | 4 |
| Mangroves* - Venezuela | 38 | 7 | 18 | 5 | 26 | 3 | 10 | 4 | 40 | 3 | 7 | 2 |
| Santa Marta montane forests - Colombia | 38 | 21 | 55 | 17 | 38 | 10 | 15 | 11 | 73 | 9 | 15 | 6 |
| Magdalena Valley montane forests - Colombia | 37 | 16 | 43 | 12 | 36 | 8 | 19 | 11 | 57 | 9 | 18 | 5 |
| Lara/Falcón dry forests - Venezuela | 36 | 8 | 22 | 7 | 26 | 4 | 8 | 3 | 37 | 3 | 7 | 2 |
| Paraguaná xeric scrub - Venezuela | 36 | 10 | 28 | 9 | 26 | 4 | 7 | 4 | 57 | 4 | 7 | 2 |
| Mangroves* - Ecuador | 34 | 7 | 21 | 4 | 20 | 4 | 7 | 4 | 57 | 3 | 3 | 2 |
| Mangroves* - Colombia | 33 | 7 | 21 | 5 | 20 | 3 | 6 | 4 | 66 | 1 | 0 | 0 |
| Guianan highlands moist forests- Venezuela, Colombia | 32 | 13 | 41 | 11 | 30 | 6 | 22 | 11 | 50 | 10 | 20 | 4 |
| Japura/Negro moist forests - Colombia, Venezuela, Peru | 32 | 14 | 44 | 11 | 30 | 7 | 21 | 12 | 57 | 10 | 19 | 6 |
| Bolivian Yungas - Bolivia, Peru | 31 | 10 | 32 | 8 | 24 | 6 | 23 | 10 | 43 | 8 | 18 | 6 |
| Peruvian Yungas - Peru | 31 | 13 | 42 | 9 | 28 | 8 | 19 | 11 | 57 | 9 | 17 | 6 |
| Varzea forests - Colombia, Ecuador, Peru | 30 | 5 | 17 | 4 | 21 | 1 | 17 | 5 | 29 | 4 | 12 | 1 |
| chaco savannas - Bolivia, Paraguay | 29 | 8 | 28 | 7 | 18 | 2 | 23 | 8 | 34 | 7 | 13 | 2 |
| Guayaquil flooded grasslands - Ecuador | 29 | 5 | 17 | 3 | 18 | 2 | 6 | 3 | 50 | 2 | 4 | 1 |
| Orinoco Delta swamp forests- Venezuela | 29 | 7 | 24 | 5 | 21 | 4 | 10 | 6 | 60 | 5 | 8 | 3 |

| Ecoregion | | | | | | | | | | | |
|---|---|---|---|---|---|---|---|---|---|---|---|
| Araya and Paría xeric scrub - Venezuela | 28 | 8 | 29 | 4 | 21 | 6 | 5 | 4 | 80 | 3 | 4 | 3 |
| Humid Chaco - Paraguay, Bolivia | 28 | 8 | 29 | 7 | 18 | 2 | 22 | 8 | 36 | 7 | 13 | 2 |
| Rondônia/Mato Grosso moist forests - Bolivia | 28 | 9 | 32 | 8 | 21 | 5 | 20 | 9 | 45 | 8 | 15 | 5 |
| Western Amazon flooded grasslands - Peru, Bolivia | 28 | 5 | 18 | 4 | 21 | 2 | 19 | 5 | 26 | 4 | 13 | 2 |
| Cauca Valley dry forests - Colombia | 27 | 7 | 26 | 5 | 23 | 4 | 8 | 3 | 37 | 2 | 6 | 2 |
| Magdalena Valley dry forests - Colombia | 27 | 8 | 30 | 5 | 25 | 6 | 9 | 5 | 55 | 3 | 8 | 4 |
| Ucayali moist forests - Peru | 27 | 12 | 44 | 10 | 23 | 6 | 21 | 11 | 52 | 10 | 17 | 5 |
| Maracaibo dry forests - Venezuela, Colombia | 26 | 10 | 38 | 9 | 22 | 5 | 11 | 6 | 54 | 6 | 8 | 3 |
| Tumbes/Piura dry forests - Ecuador, Peru | 26 | 6 | 23 | 4 | 16 | 4 | 7 | 3 | 42 | 3 | 7 | 2 |
| Beni savannas - Bolivia | 25 | 6 | 24 | 5 | 18 | 3 | 18 | 6 | 33 | 5 | 13 | 3 |
| Western Amazon swamp forests - Colombia, Peru | 25 | 6 | 24 | 5 | 19 | 3 | 17 | 6 | 35 | 5 | 12 | 3 |
| Brazilian Interior Atlantic forests - Paraguay | 24 | 7 | 29 | 6 | 17 | 2 | 19 | 7 | 36 | 6 | 14 | 2 |
| Pantanal - Bolivia, Paraguay | 24 | 6 | 25 | 5 | 16 | 2 | 19 | 6 | 31 | 5 | 12 | 2 |
| Cerrado - Paraguay, Bolivia | 23 | 6 | 26 | 5 | 18 | 3 | 17 | 6 | 35 | 5 | 13 | 3 |
| Beni swamp and gallery forests - Bolivia | 22 | 5 | 23 | 4 | 15 | 2 | 16 | 5 | 31 | 4 | 10 | 2 |
| Central Andean wet puna - Peru, Bolivia | 21 | 5 | 24 | 4 | 12 | 2 | 11 | 4 | 36 | 3 | 6 | 2 |
| Northern Andean paramo - Colombia, Ecuador, Venezuela | 21 | 3 | 14 | 3 | 15 | 2 | 12 | 3 | 25 | 3 | 8 | 2 |
| Mangroves* - Peru | 20 | 2 | 10 | 1 | 10 | 1 | 2 | 1 | 50 | 3 | 3 | 2 |
| Eastern Panamanian montane forests - Colombia | 19 | 9 | 47 | 7 | 19 | 4 | 7 | 4 | 57 | 4 | 7 | 1 |
| Bolivian lowland dry forests - Bolivia | 17 | 6 | 35 | 5 | 14 | 3 | 12 | 6 | 50 | 5 | 10 | 3 |
| Central Andean dry puna - Peru | 17 | 2 | 12 | 1 | 11 | 1 | 9 | 2 | 22 | 1 | 5 | 1 |
| Cordillera de Mérida paramo - Venezuela | 17 | 3 | 18 | 3 | 12 | 1 | 11 | 3 | 27 | 3 | 7 | 1 |
| Andean Yungas - Bolivia | 16 | 3 | 19 | 2 | 13 | 2 | 10 | 3 | 30 | 2 | 8 | 2 |
| Central Andean puna - Bolivia, Peru | 16 | 2 | 13 | 2 | 10 | 0 | 9 | 2 | 22 | 2 | 5 | 0 |
| Pelagic* - Ecuador | 16 | 7 | 44 | 5 | 5 | 3 | 7 | 4 | 57 | 3 | 3 | 2 |
| Bolivian montane dry forests - Bolivia | 14 | 3 | 21 | 2 | 11 | 2 | 8 | 3 | 37 | 2 | 6 | 2 |
| Guianan savannas - Venezuela | 14 | 4 | 29 | 3 | 11 | 2 | 11 | 4 | 36 | 3 | 9 | 2 |
| Juruá moist forests - Peru | 14 | 5 | 36 | 4 | 12 | 3 | 11 | 5 | 45 | 4 | 10 | 3 |
| Orinoco wetlands - Venezuela | 14 | 3 | 21 | 2 | 11 | 1 | 4 | 3 | 75 | 2 | 3 | 1 |
| Pelagic* - Colombia | 14 | 5 | 36 | 4 | 4 | 2 | 6 | 3 | 50 | 2 | 3 | 2 |
| Pelagic* - Peru | 13 | 6 | 46 | 4 | 5 | 3 | 6 | 4 | 66 | 3 | 3 | 2 |
| Tepuis - Venezuela | 13 | 6 | 46 | 5 | 13 | 2 | 10 | 5 | 50 | 5 | 10 | 1 |
| Patía dry forests - Colombia | 12 | 4 | 33 | 2 | 11 | 3 | 5 | 3 | 60 | 2 | 4 | 2 |
| Santa Marta paramo - Colombia | 12 | 4 | 33 | 4 | 11 | 3 | 7 | 4 | 57 | 4 | 7 | 3 |
| Cordillera Central paramo - Peru, Ecuador | 11 | 2 | 18 | 2 | 8 | 2 | 8 | 2 | 25 | 2 | 5 | 2 |
| Llanos dry forests - Venezuela | 11 | 6 | 55 | 5 | 10 | 4 | 5 | 4 | 80 | 4 | 5 | 2 |
| Macarena montane forests - Colombia | 11 | 8 | 73 | 7 | 11 | 3 | 10 | 7 | 70 | 6 | 10 | 3 |

Table

2

*Table 2.3* Distribution and Conservation Status of Neotropical Migratory Birds in Andean/Southern Cone Nations and Ecoregions (continued)

| Ecoregion[4] | All Neotropical Migrants | | | | | | Migrants with a South American Affinity | | | | | |
|---|---|---|---|---|---|---|---|---|---|---|---|---|
| | Species[4] | Cons. Concern[1] # | % | PIF[2] >18 | BBS Trends[3] # | Dec. | Species[4] | Cons. Concern[1] # | % | PIF[2] >18 | BBS Trends[3] # | Dec. |
| Paraguaná restingas - Venezuela | 9 | 2 | 22 | 2 | 4 | 1 | 1 | 1 | 100 | 1 | 1 | 1 |
| Amazonian savannas - Colombia, Venezuela | 7 | 2 | 29 | 2 | 5 | 0 | 7 | 2 | 28 | 2 | 5 | 0 |
| Pelagic* - Venezuela | 7 | 3 | 43 | 1 | 3 | 2 | 2 | 2 | 100 | 1 | 2 | 1 |
| Guianan moist forests - Venezuela | 4 | 2 | 50 | 1 | 4 | 1 | 4 | 2 | 50 | 1 | 4 | 1 |
| Marañón dry forests - Peru | 4 | 3 | 75 | 1 | 4 | 2 | 2 | 2 | 100 | 1 | 2 | 1 |

[1] Species of conservation concern: Species with PIF concern scores that are >18 and/or statistically significant negative U.S. Breeding Bird Survey (BBS) population trends.

[2] Partners in Flight (PIF) concern scores that are greater than 18.

[3] Breeding Bird Survey U.S. trend, 1966-1991. Columns indicate number of birds with trends and declines that differ significantly from zero (p<.10).

[4] Ecoregions derived from the WB/WWF Conservation Assessment (Dinerstein et al. 1995).

*This ecoregion designation was created for this study and does not conform to WB/WWF dataset.

# Table 2.4 Distribution and Conservation Status of Neotropical Migratory Birds in Parks in Peril Sites

Species richness, number (and percent) of conservation concern (as indicated by high Partners in Flight concern scores and/or US Breeding Bird Survey population declines) for all migrants and for the subset of migrants with a South American Affinity are given. See footnotes for details.

| Nation | Parks in Peril Site[1] | All Neotropical Migrants | | | | | | Migrants with a South American Affinity | | | | | |
|---|---|---|---|---|---|---|---|---|---|---|---|---|---|
| | | Species | Cons. Concern[2] # | % | PIF[3] >18 | BBS Trends[4] # | Dec. | Species | Cons. Concern[2] # | % | PIF[3] >18 | BBS Trends[4] # | Dec. |
| **Bolivia** | Amboró National Park | 41 | 15 | 36 | 13 | 30 | 7 | 31 | 15 | 48 | 13 | 23 | 7 |
| | Noel Kempff Mercado National Park | 33 | 11 | 33 | 10 | 24 | 5 | 25 | 11 | 44 | 10 | 18 | 5 |
| | Tariquia | 23 | 4 | 17 | 3 | 16 | 2 | 16 | 4 | 25 | 3 | 10 | 2 |
| **Colombia** | Sierra Nevada de Santa Marta National Park | 93 | 34 | 36 | 29 | 72 | 14 | 34 | 20 | 58 | 17 | 28 | 10 |
| | Chingaza National Park | 65 | 20 | 30 | 16 | 58 | 10 | 30 | 13 | 43 | 10 | 26 | 7 |
| | Utria National Park* | 63 | 25 | 39 | 21 | 52 | 11 | 28 | 17 | 60 | 15 | 23 | 8 |
| | La Paya National Park | 56 | 23 | 41 | 18 | 43 | 10 | 39 | 20 | 51 | 16 | 30 | 8 |
| | Cahuinari National Park | 32 | 14 | 43 | 11 | 30 | 7 | 21 | 12 | 57 | 10 | 19 | 6 |
| **Ecuador** | Machalilla National Park | 62 | 17 | 27 | 14 | 36 | 7 | 25 | 11 | 44 | 10 | 15 | 5 |
| | Antisana Ecological Reserve | 54 | 18 | 33 | 13 | 45 | 9 | 34 | 16 | 47 | 13 | 28 | 7 |
| | Cayambe-Coca Ecological Reserve | 54 | 18 | 33 | 13 | 45 | 9 | 34 | 16 | 47 | 13 | 28 | 7 |
| | Yasuni National Park | 52 | 20 | 38 | 14 | 39 | 9 | 36 | 17 | 47 | 13 | 27 | 7 |
| | Podocarpus National Park | 49 | 18 | 36 | 13 | 42 | 9 | 32 | 16 | 50 | 13 | 26 | 7 |
| | Galapagos Marine Reserve | 46 | 8 | 17 | 6 | 24 | 3 | 16 | 5 | 31 | 4 | 10 | 2 |
| | Galapagos National Park | 46 | 8 | 17 | 6 | 24 | 3 | 16 | 5 | 31 | 4 | 10 | 2 |
| | Maquipucuna | 43 | 15 | 34 | 12 | 37 | 7 | 23 | 12 | 52 | 11 | 21 | 5 |

Table

2

Table 2.4  *Distribution and Conservation Status of Neotropical Migratory Birds in Parks in Peril Sites (continued)*

| Nation | Parks in Peril Site[1] | All Neotropical Migrants | | | | | | Migrants with a South American Affinity | | | | | |
|---|---|---|---|---|---|---|---|---|---|---|---|---|---|
| | | Species | Cons. Concern[2] # | % | PIF[3] >18 | BBS Trends[4] # | Dec. | Species | Cons. Concern[2] # | % | PIF[3] >18 | BBS Trends[4] # | Dec. |
| **Paraguay** | Defensores del Chaco National Park* | 27 | 8 | 29 | 7 | 18 | 2 | 21 | 8 | 38 | 7 | 13 | 2 |
| | Mbaracayu Nature Reserve | 24 | 7 | 29 | 6 | 18 | 2 | 19 | 7 | 36 | 6 | 14 | 2 |
| **Peru** | Paracas National Reserve* | 54 | 14 | 25 | 10 | 26 | 5 | 23 | 9 | 39 | 7 | 13 | 3 |
| | Pacaya-Samiria National Reserve | 51 | 17 | 33 | 14 | 38 | 7 | 36 | 16 | 44 | 14 | 27 | 6 |
| | Tabaconas Namballe National Sanctuary | 46 | 17 | 36 | 12 | 38 | 9 | 31 | 15 | 48 | 12 | 25 | 7 |
| | Pampas del Heath National Sanctuary | 45 | 15 | 33 | 13 | 33 | 6 | 32 | 14 | 43 | 13 | 23 | 5 |
| | Yanachaga-Chemillén National Park | 39 | 16 | 41 | 11 | 34 | 9 | 27 | 14 | 51 | 11 | 23 | 7 |
| **Venezuela** | Canaima National Park | 62 | 23 | 37 | 19 | 52 | 13 | 34 | 19 | 55 | 16 | 29 | 10 |
| | Aguaro/Guariquito | 46 | 11 | 23 | 8 | 36 | 7 | 20 | 8 | 40 | 6 | 15 | 5 |

[1] = Potential Parks in Peril Site.
[2] Species of conservation concern: Species with PIF concern scores that are >18 and/or statistically significant negative U.S. Breeding Bird Survey (BBS) population trends.
[3] Partners in Flight (PIF) concern scores that are greater than 18.
[4] Breeding Bird Survey U.S. trend, 1966-1991. Columns indicate number of birds with trends and declines that differ significantly from zero (p<.10).

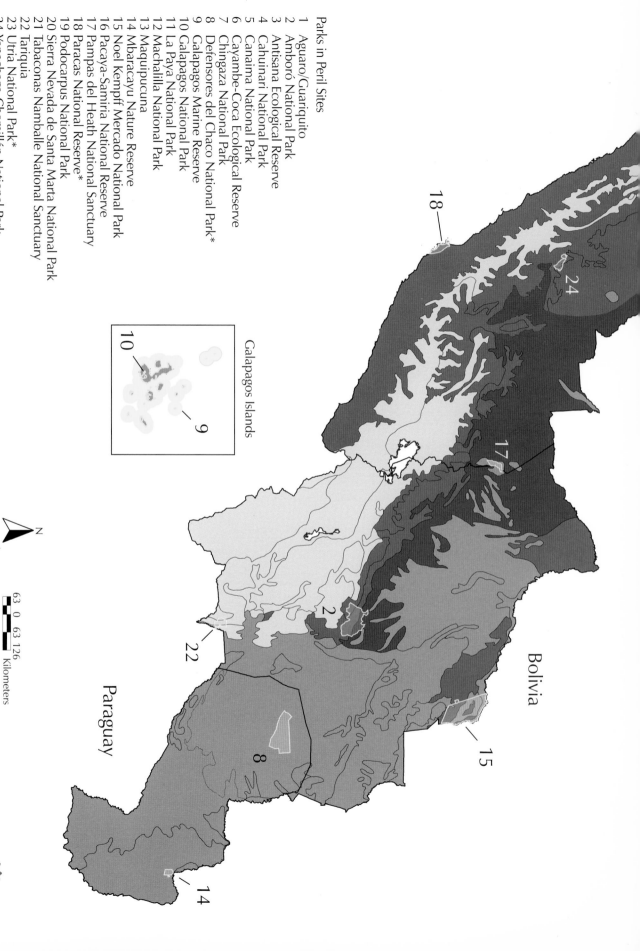

## Parks in Peril Sites

1  Aguaro/Guariquito
2  Amboró National Park
3  Antisana Ecological Reserve
4  Cahuinari National Park
5  Canaima National Park
6  Cayambe-Coca Ecological Reserve
7  Chingaza National Park
8  Defensores del Chaco National Park*
9  Galapagos Marine Reserve
10 Galapagos National Park
11 La Paya National Park
12 Machalilla National Park
13 Maquipucuna
14 Mbaracayu Nature Reserve
15 Noel Kempff Mercado National Park
16 Pacaya-Samiria National Reserve
17 Pampas del Heath National Sanctuary
18 Paracas National Reserve*
19 Podocarpus National Park
20 Sierra Nevada de Santa Marta National Park
21 Tabaconas Namballe National Sanctuary
22 Tariquia
23 Utria National Park
24 Yanachaga-Chemillén National Park
25 Yasuni National Park*
* Potential Parks in Peril Site

Galapagos Islands

10

9

Bolivia

Paraguay

N

63 0 63 126 Kilometers

Data sources: Ecoregions developed by World Bank / World Wildlife Fund (Dinerstein et al. 1995).
Neotropical migratory bird occurrences compiled by TNC's Migratory Bird Information System.
Species of Conservation Concern: Species with Partners in Flight concern scores >18 and/or
statistically significant US Breeding Bird Survey population declines 1966-1991.
Parks in Peril is a program designed by TNC for the protection of threatened areas in
Latin America and the Caribbean.
Political boundaries derived from ESRI's Digital Chart of the World.

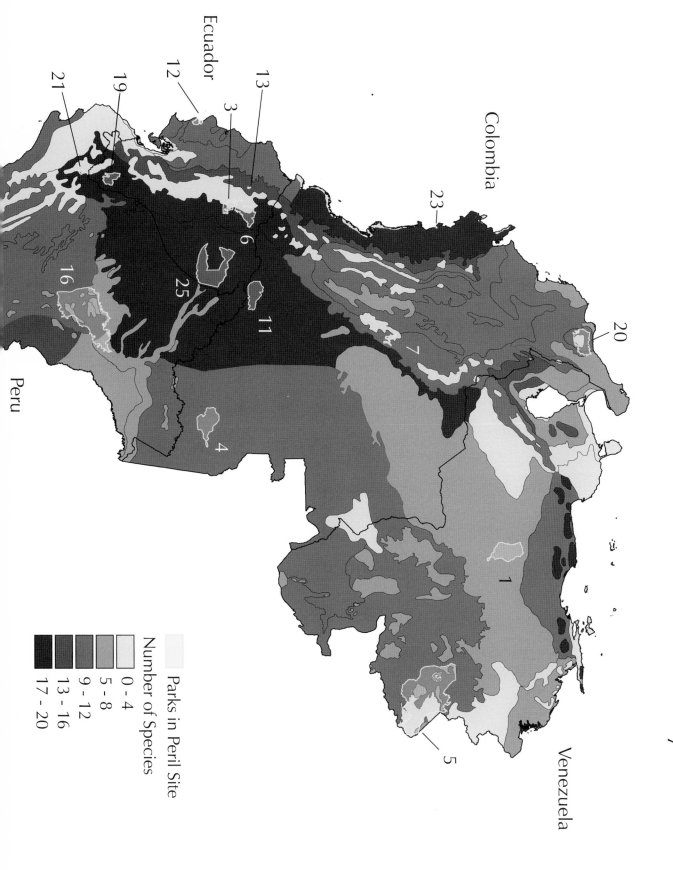

Figure 2.5 Species Richness in Ecoregions: Migrants of Conservation Concern with a South American Affinity

Parks in Peril Site

Number of Species
0 - 4
5 - 8
9 - 12
13 - 16
17 - 20

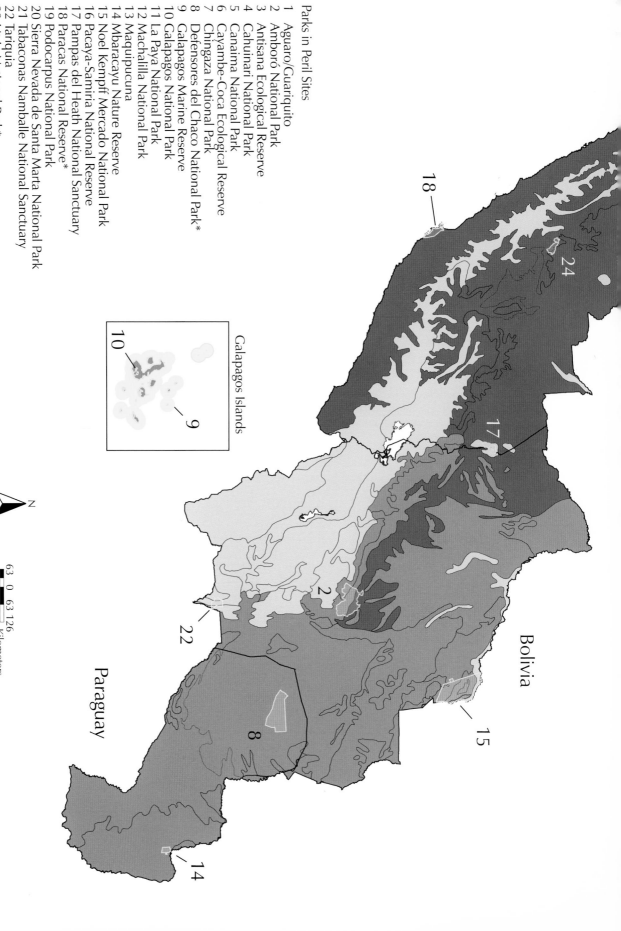

Parks in Peril Sites
1 Aguaro/Guariquito
2 Amboró National Park
3 Antisana Ecological Reserve
4 Cahuinari National Park
5 Canaima National Park
6 Cayambe-Coca Ecological Reserve
7 Chingaza National Park
8 Defensores del Chaco National Park*
9 Galapagos Marine Reserve
10 Galapagos National Park
11 La Paya National Park
12 Machalilla National Park
13 Maquipucuna
14 Mbaracayu Nature Reserve
15 Noel Kempff Mercado National Park
16 Pacaya-Samiria National Reserve
17 Pampas del Heath National Sanctuary
18 Paracas National Reserve*
19 Podocarpus National Park
20 Sierra Nevada de Santa Marta National Park
21 Tabaconas Namballe National Sanctuary
22 Tariquia
23 Utria National Park*
24 Yanachaga-Chemillén National Park
25 Yasuni National Park
* Potential Parks in Peril Site

Galapagos Islands

10

9

N

63 0 63 126
Kilometers

Data sources: Ecoregions developed by World Bank / World Wildlife Fund (Dinerstein et al. 1995).
Neotropical migratory bird occurrences compiled by TNC's Migratory Bird Information System.
Species of Conservation Concern: Species with Partners in Flight concern scores > 18 and/or
statistically significant US Breeding Bird Survey population declines 1966-1991.
Parks in Peril is a program designed by TNC for the protection of threatened areas in
Latin America and the Caribbean.
Political boundaries derived from ESRI's Digital Chart of the World.

Bolivia

17

24

18

15

2

22

8

14

Paraguay

The Nature Conservancy®

WWF

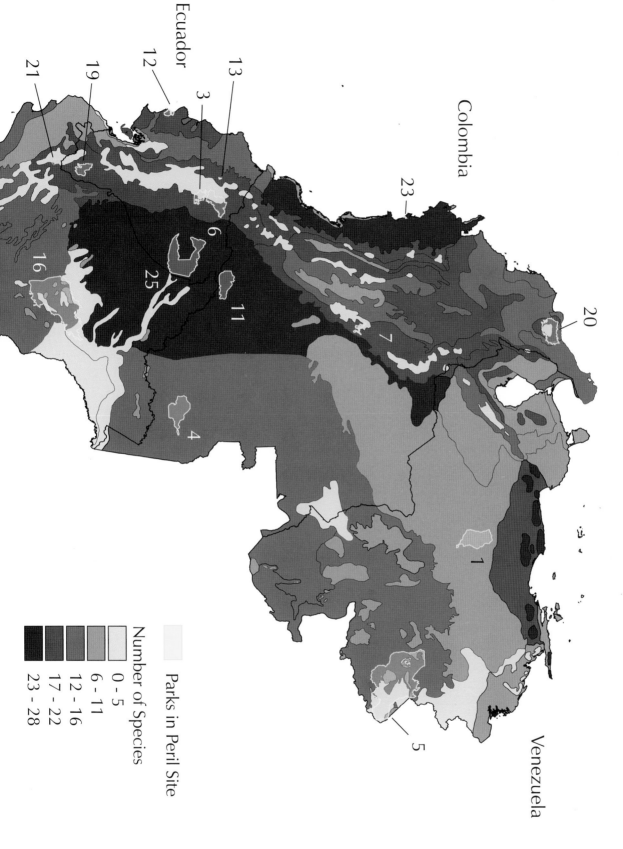

Figure 2.4 Species Richness in Ecoregions:
Migrants of Conservation Concern

Parks in Peril Site

Number of Species
0 - 5
6 - 11
12 - 16
17 - 22
23 - 28

# Figure 2.3 Species Richness in Ecoregions: Migrants with a South American Affinity

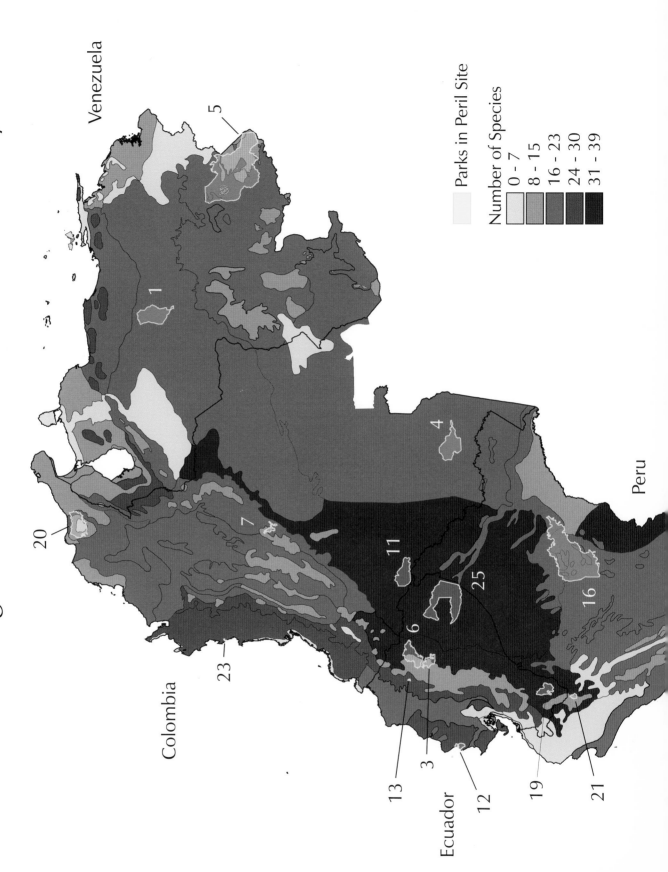

Parks in Peril Site

Number of Species
0 - 7
8 - 15
16 - 23
24 - 30
31 - 39

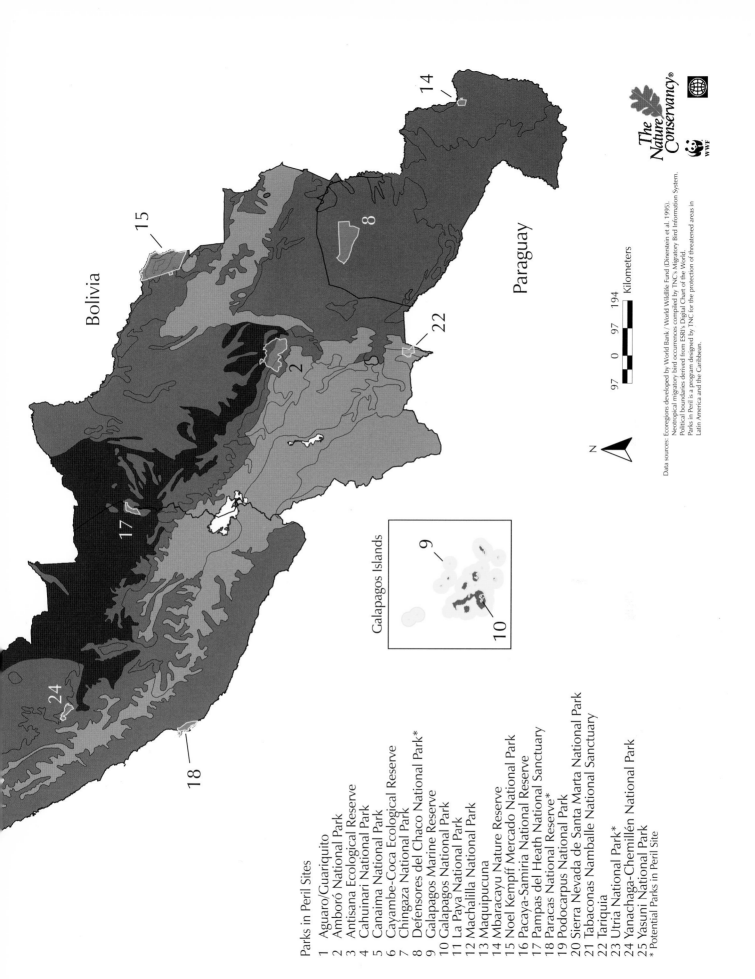

Bolivia

Paraguay

Galapagos Islands

14

15

8

22

2

5

17

24

18

9

10

N

97   0   97   194
Kilometers

Data sources: Ecoregions developed by World Bank / World Wildlife Fund (Dinerstein et al. 1995).
Neotropical migratory bird occurrences compiled by TNC's Migratory Bird Information System.
Political boundaries derived from ESRI's Digital Chart of the World.
Parks in Peril is a program designed by TNC for the protection of threatened areas in
Latin America and the Caribbean.

The Nature Conservancy®

WWF

Parks in Peril Sites

1   Aguaro/Guariquito
2   Amboró National Park
3   Antisana Ecological Reserve
4   Cahuinari National Park
5   Canaima National Park
6   Cayambe-Coca Ecological Reserve
7   Chingaza National Park
8   Defensores del Chaco National Park*
9   Galapagos Marine Reserve
10  Galapagos National Park
11  La Paya National Park
12  Machalilla National Park
13  Maquipucuna
14  Mbaracayu Nature Reserve
15  Noel Kempff Mercado National Park
16  Pacaya-Samiria National Reserve
17  Pampas del Heath National Sanctuary
18  Paracas National Reserve*
19  Podocarpus National Park
20  Sierra Nevada de Santa Marta National Park
21  Tabaconas Namballe National Sanctuary
22  Tariquia
23  Utria National Park*
24  Yanachaga-Chemillén National Park
25  Yasuni National Park
*   Potential Parks in Peril Site

# Figure 2.2 Species Richness in Ecoregion: All Neotropical Migrants

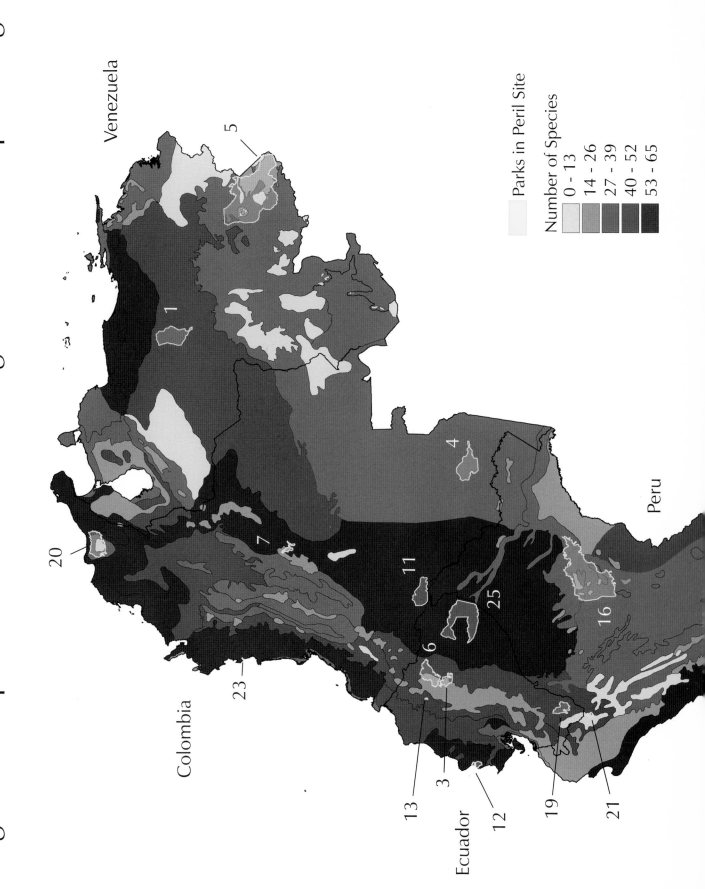

Venezuela

Colombia

Ecuador

Peru

Parks in Peril Site

Number of Species

0 - 13
14 - 26
27 - 39
40 - 52
53 - 65

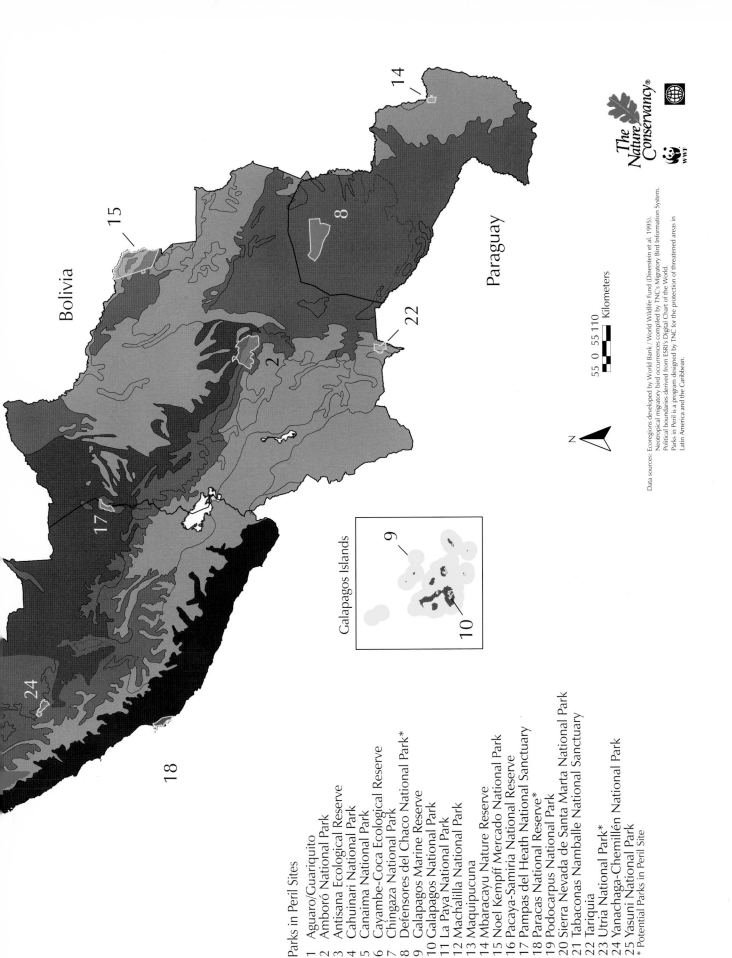

Bolivia

Paraguay

14

15

8

22

2

17

18

24

Galapagos Islands

9

10

N

55  0  55  110
Kilometers

Data sources: Ecoregions developed by World Bank / World Wildlife Fund (Dinerstein et al. 1995).
Neotropical migratory bird occurrences compiled by TNC's Migratory Bird Information System.
Political boundaries derived from ESRI's Digital Chart of the World.
Parks in Peril is a program designed by TNC for the protection of threatened areas in
Latin America and the Caribbean.

The Nature Conservancy®

WWF

Parks in Peril Sites

1  Aguaro/Guariquito
2  Amboró National Park
3  Antisana Ecological Reserve
4  Cahuinari National Park
5  Canaima National Park
6  Cayambe-Coca Ecological Reserve
7  Chingaza National Park
8  Defensores del Chaco National Park*
9  Galapagos Marine Reserve
10  Galapagos National Park
11  La Paya National Park
12  Machalilla National Park
13  Maquipucuna
14  Mbaracayu Nature Reserve
15  Noel Kempff Mercado National Park
16  Pacaya-Samiria National Reserve
17  Pampas del Heath National Sanctuary
18  Paracas National Reserve*
19  Podocarpus National Park
20  Sierra Nevada de Santa Marta National Park
21  Tabaconas Namballe National Sanctuary
22  Tariquia
23  Utria National Park*
24  Yanachaga-Chemillén National Park
25  Yasuni National Park
*  Potential Parks in Peril Site

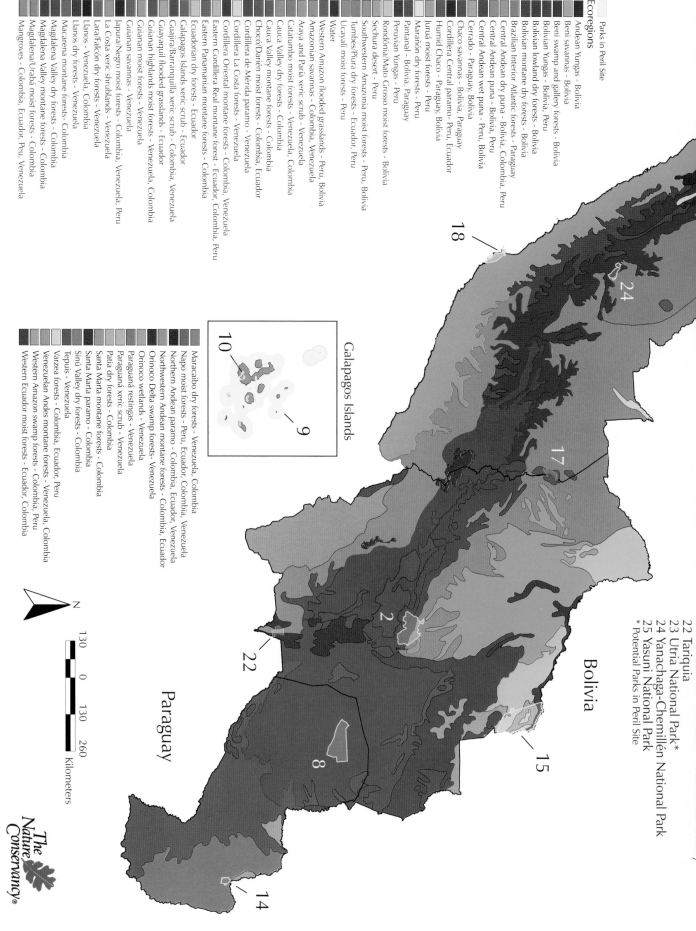

Parks in Peril Site

Ecoregions

Andean Yungas - Bolivia
Beni savannas - Bolivia
Beni swamp and gallery forests - Bolivia
Bolivian Yungas - Bolivia, Peru
Bolivian Yungas - Bolivia
Bolivian lowland dry forests - Bolivia
Bolivian montane dry forests - Bolivia
Brazilian Interior Atlantic forests - Paraguay
Central Andean dry puna - Bolivia, Chile, Peru
Central Andean puna - Bolivia, Peru
Central Andean wet puna - Peru, Bolivia
Cerrado - Bolivia, Brazil
Cerrado - Paraguay, Bolivia
Chaco savannas - Bolivia, Paraguay
Cordillera Central paramo - Peru, Ecuador
Humid Chaco - Paraguay, Bolivia
Jurúa moist forests - Peru
Marañón dry forests - Peru
Pantanal - Bolivia, Paraguay
Peruvian Yungas - Peru
Rondônia/Mato Grosso moist forests - Bolivia
Sechura desert - Peru
Southwestern Amazonia moist forests - Peru, Peru, Bolivia
Tumbes/Piura dry forests - Ecuador, Peru
Ucayali moist forests - Peru
Water
Western Amazon flooded grasslands - Peru, Bolivia
Amazonian savannas - Colombia, Venezuela
Araya and Paría xeric scrub - Venezuela
Catatumbo moist forests - Venezuela, Colombia
Cauca Valley dry forests - Colombia
Cauca Valley montane forests - Colombia
Chocó/Darién moist forests - Colombia, Ecuador
Cordillera de Mérida paramo - Venezuela
Cordillera La Costa forests - Venezuela
Cordillera Oriental montane forests - Colombia, Venezuela
Eastern Cordillera Real montane forest - Ecuador, Colombia, Peru
Eastern Panamanian montane forests - Colombia
Ecuadorian dry forests - Ecuador
Galapagos Islands xeric scrub - Ecuador
Guajira/Barranquilla xeric scrub - Colombia, Venezuela
Guayaquil flooded grasslands - Ecuador
Guianan highlands moist forests - Venezuela, Colombia
Guianan moist forests - Venezuela
Guianan savannas - Venezuela
Japurá/Negro moist forests - Colombia, Venezuela, Peru
La Costa xeric shrublands - Venezuela
Lara/Falcón dry forests - Venezuela
Llanos - Venezuela, Colombia
Llanos dry forests - Venezuela
Macarena montane forests - Colombia
Magdalena Valley dry forests - Colombia
Magdalena Valley montane forests - Colombia
Magdalena/Urabá moist forests - Colombia
Mangroves - Colombia, Ecuador, Peru, Venezuela

Galapagos Islands

10
9

Maracaibo dry forests - Venezuela, Colombia
Napo moist forests - Peru, Ecuador, Colombia, Venezuela
Northern Andean paramo - Colombia, Ecuador, Venezuela
Northwestern Andean montane forests - Colombia, Ecuador
Orinoco Delta swamp forests - Venezuela
Orinoco wetlands - Colombia, Ecuador
Paraguaná restingas - Venezuela
Paraguaná xeric scrub - Venezuela
Patía dry forests - Colombia
Santa Marta montane forests - Colombia
Santa Marta paramo - Colombia
Sinú Valley dry forests - Colombia
Tepuis - Venezuela
Varzea forests - Colombia, Ecuador, Peru
Venezuelan Andes montane forests - Venezuela, Colombia
Western Amazon swamp forests - Colombia, Peru
Western Ecuador moist forests - Ecuador, Colombia

18
24
17
2
22
15
8
14

22 Tariquia
23 Utria National Park*
24 Yanachaga-Chemillén National Park
25 Yasuní National Park
* Potential Parks in Peril Site

Bolivia

Paraguay

N

130    0    130    260
Kilometers

The Nature Conservancy®

WWF

Data sources: Ecoregions developed by World Bank / World Wildlife Fund (Dinerstein et al. 1995).
Political boundaries derived from ESRI's Digital Chart of the World.
Parks in Peril is a program designed by TNC for the protection of threatened areas in Latin America and the Caribbean.

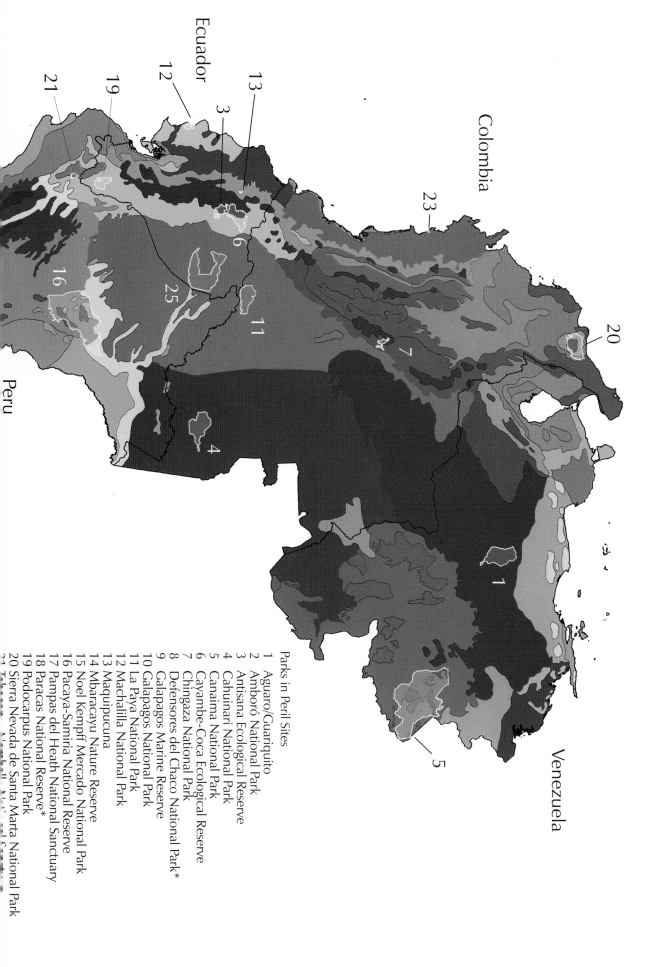

**Figure 2.1  Ecoregions and Parks in Peril Sites of the Andean/Southern Cone Region**

Parks in Peril Sites

1   Aguaro/Guariquito
2   Amboró National Park
3   Antisana Ecological Reserve
4   Cahuinari National Park
5   Canaima National Park
6   Cayambe-Coca Ecological Reserve
7   Chingaza National Park
8   Defensores del Chaco National Park*
9   Galapagos Marine Reserve
10  Galapagos National Park
11  La Paya National Park
12  Machalilla National Park
13  Maquipucuna
14  Mbaracayu Nature Reserve
15  Noel Kempff Mercado National Park
16  Pacaya-Samiria National Reserve
17  Pampas del Heath National Sanctuary
18  Paracas National Reserve*
19  Podocarpus National Park
20  Sierra Nevada de Santa Marta National Park

# Chapter 3

# *National Assessments*

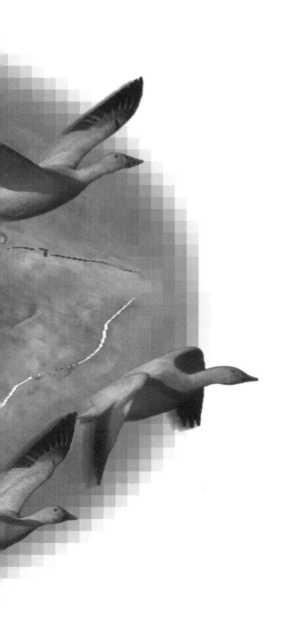

One of the primary objectives of this study is to spotlight the conservation status and distribution of migrants for the six nations of the ASC Region. Another purpose is to enhance local conservation initiatives by linking U.S. and Latin American efforts through the Conservancy's Migratory Bird Initiative and Parks in Peril program.

To address these objectives, a quick sketch of each nation's natural history will be followed by an overview of its neotropical migratory birds, migrants with a South American affinity, and Parks in Peril sites. Each discussion concludes with an analysis of the numbers of migrants of conservation concern.

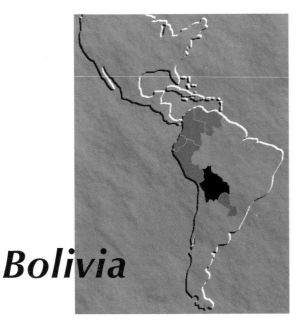

# Bolivia

Jaguars prowl through the dark forests of Bolivia, sword-nosed bats dart through its skies, and awesome black caymans swim through its swamps. From the Amazon basin forests that compose two-thirds of Bolivia to its savannas, chaco, and swamp forests, across the Andes and yungas to the puna in the west, the habitats of this country teem with biological diversity.

Bolivia is also a nation of unique natural landscapes. High above its forests is a lake that was sacred to the Incas. The Titicaca Lake, the highest navigable lake on Earth, harbors many endemic and Andean species. Of the 16 ecoregions in Bolivia's 1,098,575 square kilometers, the Beni savannas, Beni swamp and gallery forests, Bolivian lowland forests, and Bolivian montane dry forests are unique to the nation. (See Figure 3.1.)

Bolivia may be one of the most environmentally undamaged nations in South America due to the relatively low density of its human population. The population is concentrated mainly in the southwestern part of the country. Nevertheless, Bolivia is under constant

attack and threat from loggers, hunters, and illegal settlers seeking to exploit its valuable resources.

Approximately half of Bolivia is still forested, mostly in the Amazonian lowlands. Roughly 20 percent of the Andean slopes also remain wooded.[32] Some of the country's rich flora and fauna are preserved in its 25 protected areas.[33]

With about 1,358 species of birds,[34] Bolivia is the richest landlocked nation in the world in terms of bird diversity. The country harbors 43 neotropical migrants that put in a regular appearance. (See Tables 2.3 and 3.7.) The southwestern Amazonia moist forests host the greatest number of migratory species. (See Table 3.1 and Figure 3.2.) Incidentally, this region is part of the high rainfall zone that extends northward into the area where the Amazonian forests meet the Andean foothills. This area is considered by Ridgely and Tudor to have the highest avian diversity of any region of the world.[35] Other ecoregions with high species richness are the Bolivian yungas (with high endemism and species richness), chaco savannas (supporting many regional endemics and habitat types), and the Rondônia/Mato Grosso moist forests (supporting many endemic species).[36]

Bolivia harbors 33 species of neotropical migrants with a South American affinity. (See Tables 2.3 and 3.7.) As with migrants in general, the highest numbers of these species occur in the central portion of the nation: the southwestern Amazonia moist forests, Bolivian yungas, and the chaco savannas. (See Table 3.1 and Figure 3.2.)

The eastern kingbird relies primarily on the Amazonian region of eastern Bolivia during the nonbreeding season. This tyrant flycatcher lives up to the "tyrant" of its name, for it has been known to attack

*The eastern kingbird, a neotropical migrant found virtually everywhere in Bolivia, is known for its brazen attacks on hawks, crows, and vultures—and even one foray against a low-flying air plane. Bolivia's unique habitats are threatened by loggers, hunters, and illegal settlers.*

hawks, crows, and vultures brazenly, and one kingbird even went after a low-flying airplane crossing its territory.[37] The bird can occur virtually anywhere in the country during its time in Bolivia, but it usually chooses forest canopies, humid forest, and secondary woodland borders. The eastern kingbird generally does not sing its raspy call while it is on its nonbreeding grounds but instead remains unusually silent.

Three Parks in Peril sites are located in the middle, eastern, and southern parts of the nation and overlay nine ecoregions. (See Table 2.4 and Figure 3.1.) The sites represent three of the five ecoregions that are unique to Bolivia: the Beni savannas and the Beni swamp and gallery forests.

In the center of the nation is Amboró National Park, located in humid yungas and lowlands. It is one of the nation's richest parks topographically. To the northeast is

Noel Kempff Mercado National Park, where unique habitat transition zones have created a distinctive mixture of cerrado, evergreen, and gallery forests. To the south, Tariquia's domain is high in the mountains and mostly forested with a monsoon-like climate.[38] All three sites harbor at least 23 migratory species each; one site has an estimated 41 species. (See Tables 2.4 and 3.7.)

Bolivia provides nonbreeding habitat for 16 migratory species of conservation concern, all of which are migrants with a South American affinity. (See Tables 2.3 and 3.7.) The ecoregions with the highest species richness for this group are the southwestern Amazonia moist forests, Bolivian yungas, and the Rondônia/Mato Grosso moist forests. (See Table 3.1 and Figure 3.3.)

Bolivia also provides nonbreeding habitat for the six species singled out in Chapter 2 as having an uncertain future according to outside studies: broad-winged hawk, Swainson's hawk, American golden-plover, upland sandpiper, barn swallow, and yellow-green vireo. The prospect for these 22 species (the six listed plus the 16 species of conservation concern that have a South American affinity) depends in part on the future of their habitats in Bolivia. Conservation planners in Bolivia should attempt to integrate the habitat needs of these species with other important biodiversity data when designing reserve systems.

## Table 3.1 Distribution and Conservation Status of Neotropical Migratory Birds in Bolivia

Species richness, number (and percent) of conservation concern (as indicated by high Partners in Flight concern scores and/or US Breeding Bird Survey population declines) for all migrants and for the subset of migrants with a South American Affinity are given. See footnotes for details.

| Ecoregions[4] | All Neotropical Migrants | | | | | | Migrants with a South American Affinity | | | | | |
|---|---|---|---|---|---|---|---|---|---|---|---|---|
| | Species | Cons. Concern[1] # | % | PIF[2] >18 | BBS Trends[3] # | Dec. | Species | Cons. Concern[1] # | % | PIF[2] >18 | BBS Trends[3] # | Dec. |
| Southwestern Amazonia moist forests | 37 | 13 | 35 | 12 | 27 | 5 | 29 | 13 | 44 | 12 | 21 | 5 |
| Bolivian Yungas | 31 | 10 | 32 | 8 | 24 | 6 | 23 | 10 | 43 | 8 | 18 | 6 |
| Chaco savannas | 27 | 7 | 25 | 6 | 18 | 2 | 21 | 7 | 33 | 6 | 13 | 2 |
| Rondônia/Mato Grosso moist forests | 27 | 9 | 33 | 8 | 20 | 5 | 20 | 9 | 45 | 8 | 15 | 5 |
| Humid Chaco | 26 | 7 | 26 | 6 | 18 | 2 | 20 | 7 | 35 | 6 | 13 | 2 |
| Beni savannas | 25 | 6 | 24 | 5 | 17 | 3 | 18 | 6 | 33 | 5 | 13 | 3 |
| Western Amazon flooded grasslands | 25 | 5 | 20 | 4 | 18 | 2 | 18 | 5 | 27 | 4 | 12 | 2 |
| Pantanal | 24 | 6 | 25 | 5 | 16 | 2 | 19 | 6 | 31 | 5 | 12 | 2 |
| Cerrado | 23 | 6 | 26 | 5 | 18 | 3 | 17 | 6 | 35 | 5 | 13 | 3 |
| Beni swamp and gallery forests | 22 | 5 | 22 | 4 | 15 | 2 | 16 | 5 | 31 | 4 | 10 | 2 |
| Bolivian lowland dry forests | 17 | 6 | 35 | 5 | 14 | 3 | 12 | 6 | 50 | 5 | 10 | 3 |
| Central Andean wet puna | 17 | 3 | 17 | 2 | 11 | 2 | 10 | 3 | 30 | 2 | 6 | 2 |
| Andean Yungas | 16 | 3 | 18 | 2 | 13 | 2 | 10 | 3 | 30 | 2 | 8 | 2 |
| Central Andean dry puna | 15 | 2 | 13 | 1 | 11 | 1 | 9 | 2 | 22 | 1 | 5 | 1 |
| Central Andean puna | 15 | 2 | 13 | 2 | 10 | 0 | 9 | 2 | 22 | 2 | 5 | 0 |
| Bolivian montane dry forests | 14 | 3 | 21 | 2 | 11 | 2 | 8 | 3 | 37 | 2 | 6 | 2 |

[1] Species of conservation concern: Species with PIF concern scores that are >18 and/or statistically significant negative U.S. Breeding Bird Survey (BBS) population trends.
[2] Partners in Flight (PIF) concern scores that are greater than 18.
[3] Breeding Bird Survey U.S. trend, 1966-1991. Columns indicate number of birds with trends and declines that differ significantly from zero (p<.10).
[4] Ecoregions derived from the WB/WWF Conservation Assessment (Dinerstein et al. 1995).

Table 3

65

# Figure 3.1 Ecoregions and Parks in Peril Sites of Bolivia

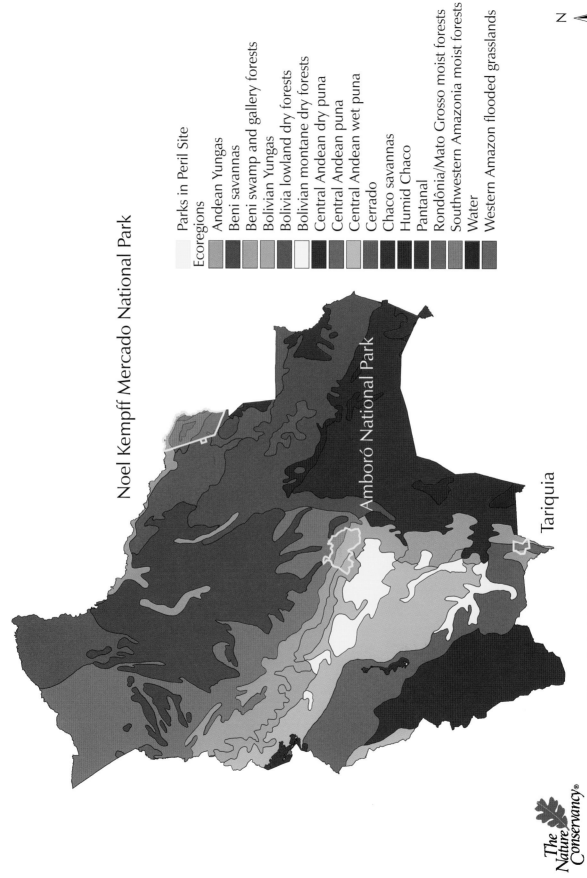

Noel Kempff Mercado National Park

Amboró National Park

Tariquia

Parks in Peril Site

Ecoregions
- Andean Yungas
- Beni savannas
- Beni swamp and gallery forests
- Bolivian Yungas
- Bolivia lowland dry forests
- Bolivian montane dry forests
- Central Andean dry puna
- Central Andean puna
- Central Andean wet puna
- Cerrado
- Chaco savannas
- Humid Chaco
- Pantanal
- Rondônia/Mato Grosso moist forests
- Southwestern Amazonia moist forests
- Water
- Western Amazon flooded grasslands

N

96    0    96    192
Kilometers

Data sources: Ecoregions developed by World Bank / World Wildlife Fund (Dinerstein et al. 1995).
Political boundaries derived from ESRI's Digital Chart of the World.
Parks in Peril is a program designed by TNC for the protection of threatened areas in Latin America and the Caribbean.

The Nature Conservancy®

WWF

# Figure 3.2  Migrant Species Richness in Ecoregions of Bolivia

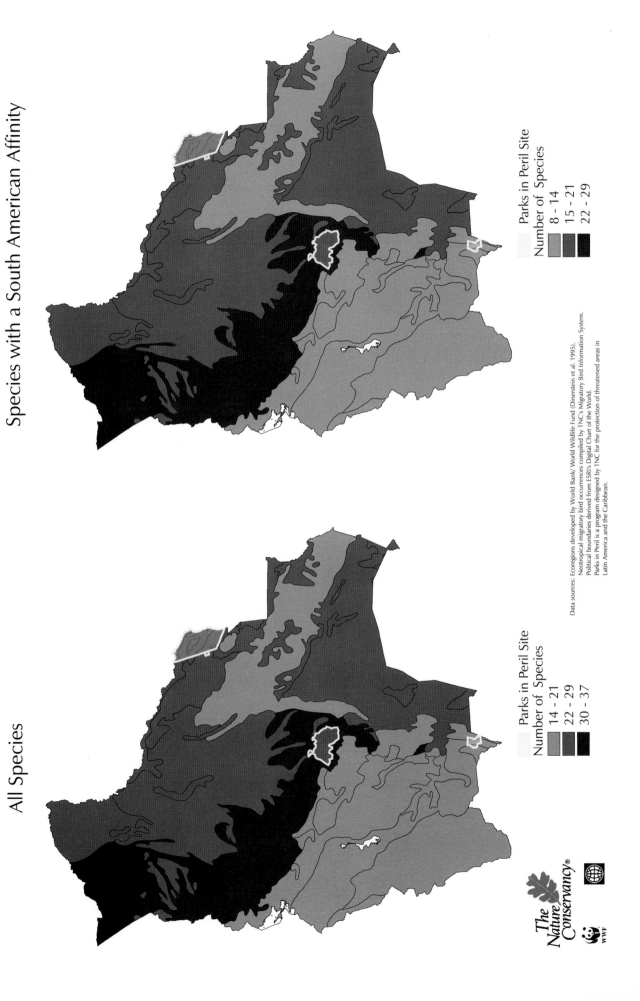

### Species with a South American Affinity

Parks in Peril Site

Number of  Species
- 8 - 14
- 15 - 21
- 22 - 29

### All Species

Parks in Peril Site

Number of  Species
- 14 - 21
- 22 - 29
- 30 - 37

Data sources: Ecoregions developed by World Bank/ World Wildlife Fund (Dinerstein et al. 1995).
Neotropical migratory bird occurrences compiled by TNC's Migratory Bird Information System.
Political boundaries derived from ESRI's Digital Chart of the World.
Parks in Peril is a program designed by TNC for the protection of threatened areas in
Latin America and the Caribbean.

# Figure 3.3  Migrant Species Richness in Ecoregions of Bolivia:
## Species of Conservation Concern

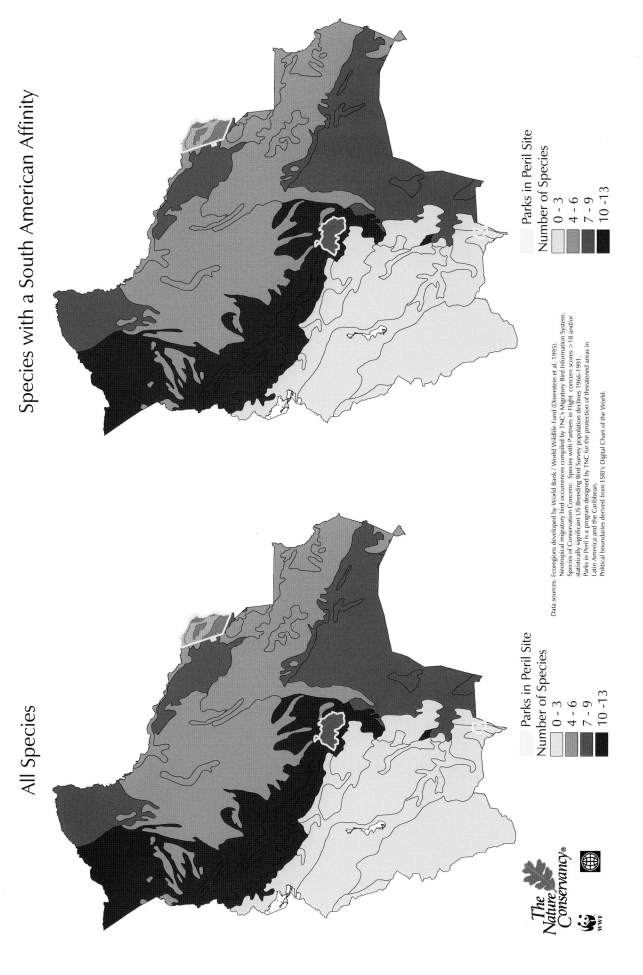

Species with a South American Affinity

All Species

Parks in Peril Site

Number of Species
- 0 - 3
- 4 - 6
- 7 - 9
- 10 -13

Data sources: Ecoregions developed by World Bank / World Wildlife Fund (Dinerstein et al. 1995).
Neotropical migratory bird occurrences compiled by TNC's Migratory Bird Information System.
Species of Conservation Concern:  Species with Partners in Flight concern scores > 18 and/or
statistically significant US Breeding Bird Survey population declines 1966-1991.
Parks in Peril is a program designed by TNC for the protection of threatened areas in
Latin America and the Caribbean.
Political boundaries derived from ESRI's Digital Chart of the World.

# *Colombia*

Where the blue waters of the Caribbean lap against Colombia's shores, a vertical massif rises 18,000 feet to culminate in two snow-covered peaks. Among the most amazing geological formations in the Americas is Colombia's isolated Sierra Nevada de Santa Marta. Pyramid-shaped, it emerges abruptly from the flat Caribbean plain. Starting at sea level, each gain in altitude leads to another ecoregion: dry forests, then moist forests, next the tundra-like paramo, and finally glaciers. The twin peaks of the massif, which was present before the Andes rose, are the Pico Simón Bolívar and Pico Cristobal. They are the highest in Colombia.

Colombia has perhaps the most complex topography in South America. The eastern half of the nation is flat, but the western region includes a complex series of three mountain ranges oriented north to south. The three ranges are the eastern, central, and western Andes.

With such varied topography, Colombia's 1,138,907 square kilometers have 30 ecoregions. (See Figure 3.4.) They include montane forests, moist forests of the Chocó, mangroves, Napo moist forests, the Japura/Negro region, varzea habitats, Amazon swamp forests, Andean forests, submontane forests of the valleys, dry forests, Amazonian savannas, the llanos, paramos, and other areas. These diverse habitats harbor one of the richest avifauna of South America, encompassing more than 1,700 species.[39]

The complex array of Colombian ecosystems has received increased national and international attention directed at improving the protection of this unique biodiversity. Large portions of the Pacific slope, the eastern slope of the eastern Andes, and the lowlands east of the Andes are still relatively undisturbed. Currently, Colombia has 79 protected areas.[40] Conversely, deforestation is occurring at an alarming rate in the central mountain region and across most of northern Colombia. In addition, the loss of forest is expanding into other portions of the Andes.[41]

Of the nation's 30 ecoregions, 10 are unique to Colombia. Among them are the Macarena montane forests, Magdalena/Urabá moist forests, and the Cauca Valley montane forests. (See Figure 3.4.) The mountains and lowlands of the central region and eastern coast are the areas with the highest species richness. (See Table 3.2 and Figure 3.5.) The Chocó/Darién moist forests ecoregion is the most species-rich region of Colombia. This is not surprising, for the Chocó is considered to possess the world's richest lowland biotas with exceptional biodiversity in a wide range of taxa.[42] The Chocó also is regarded as an "exceptionally species-rich" endemic center.[43] Other species-rich ecoregions are the Guajira/Barranquilla xeric scrub, Sinú Valley dry forests, and the Napo moist forests, which contain one of the richest biotas in the world.[44]

*The Blackburnian warbler, which makes its home in the montane forests of Colombia during the nonbreeding season, is particularly vulnerable to deforestation. Forests in Colombia's central mountain region and other portions of the Andes are especially hard-hit.*

Of the six nations of the ASC Region, Colombia hosts the largest number (131 species) of neotropical migrants. (See Tables 2.3 and 3.7.) The explanation perhaps is in part due to Colombia's location at the end of the Central American "arm." Indeed, northern migrants constitute a significant proportion of the total avifauna of Colombia. This is particularly true of shorebirds, which are numerous on both coasts.[45]

All of the 53 neotropical migrants with a South American affinity occur in Colombia. This nation should be considered a priority in terms of promoting the conservation of this unique group of migrants. (See Tables 2.3 and 3.7.) Colombian ecoregions with the highest number of migrants with a South American affinity include the Napo moist forests, eastern Cordillera Real montane forests, and the Chocó/Darién moist forests. (See Table 3.2. and Figure 3.5.)

One of the species with a South American affinity that makes its home in these ecoregions during the nonbreeding season is the Blackburnian warbler. The male's radiant bright orange throat and head markings make this bird a beauty to behold. The Blackburnian warbler is a species with nonbreeding site fidelity, meaning that it returns annually to the same locale. As a common nonbreeding resident of the forests and especially the montane regions of Colombia, the Blackburnian warbler is easily the most numerous of northern warblers in the Colombian Andes.[46] It is particularly vulnerable to deforestation, and it has a high Partners in Flight score.

Four Parks in Peril sites and one potential site (Utria National Park) are located in the northern, western, central, and southern parts of Colombia and overlay nine ecoregions. (See Table 2.4 and Figure 3.4.) Three of these ecoregions—the Santa Marta paramo, Santa Marta montane forests, and the Sinú Valley dry forests—are found only in Colombia.

In the north, Sierra Nevada de Santa Marta National Park is located on the highest seaside mountain on earth.[47] Within its boundaries are tropical moist forests, paramo, and even permanently snow-covered peaks. To the southwest is Utria National Park, situated in the heart of the rich lowland wet forest of the Chocó. East of Utria, cradled in mountains, rolling hills, and ravines, is Chingaza National Park, which protects several important watersheds. The fourth site, La Paya National Park, is situated in the lowland Amazonian plains and is known for its great botanical diversity. To the east, in the Amazonian basin, is Cahuinari National Park, which abounds with rivers. All five Parks in Peril sites in Colombia host at least 32 migratory species each; one site has an estimated 93 species. (See Tables 2.4 and 3.7.)

Colombia harbors 47 species of conservation concern. Almost two-thirds (29 species) of these are migrants with a South American affinity. (See Tables 2.3 and 3.7.) The highest species richness for both the 47 species and the South American affinity subgroup occurs in the Chocó/Darién moist forests, Catatumbo and Napo moist forests, and the eastern Cordillera Real montane forests. (See Figure 3.6.)

An additional group mentioned in Chapter 2 includes six species with tenuous futures: broad-winged hawk, Swainson's hawk, American golden-plover, upland sandpiper, barn swallow, and yellow-green vireo. Information on the habitat needs of these 35 species for which Colombia is so important should be integrated with parallel information on resident avian species (including endemics) as a national conservation strategy is developed.

# Table 3.2 Distribution and Conservation Status of Neotropical Migratory Birds in Colombia

Species richness, number (and percent) of conservation concern (as indicated by high Partners in Flight concern scores and/or US Breeding Bird Survey population declines) for all migrants and for the subset of migrants with a South American Affinity are given. See footnotes for details.

| | All Neotropical Migrants | | | | | | Migrants with a South American Affinity | | | | | |
| Ecoregions[4] | Species | Cons. Concern[1] # | % | PIF[2] >18 | BBS Trends[3] # | Dec. | Species | Cons. Concern[1] # | % | PIF[2] >18 | BBS Trends[3] # | Dec. |
|---|---|---|---|---|---|---|---|---|---|---|---|---|
| Chocó/Darién moist forests | 63 | 25 | 39 | 21 | 52 | 11 | 28 | 17 | 60 | 15 | 23 | 8 |
| Guajira/Barranquilla xeric scrub | 61 | 13 | 21 | 12 | 41 | 5 | 15 | 7 | 46 | 6 | 9 | 4 |
| Sinú Valley dry forests | 57 | 16 | 28 | 14 | 45 | 8 | 16 | 9 | 56 | 8 | 14 | 5 |
| Napo moist forests | 56 | 23 | 41 | 18 | 43 | 10 | 39 | 20 | 51 | 16 | 30 | 8 |
| Cordillera Oriental montane forests | 53 | 18 | 33 | 14 | 51 | 9 | 23 | 11 | 47 | 8 | 22 | 6 |
| Eastern Cordillera Real montane forest | 52 | 20 | 38 | 15 | 44 | 10 | 33 | 17 | 51 | 14 | 27 | 7 |
| Northwestern Andean montane forests | 49 | 19 | 38 | 16 | 43 | 8 | 24 | 13 | 54 | 12 | 21 | 5 |
| Catatumbo moist forests | 48 | 22 | 45 | 19 | 43 | 10 | 25 | 14 | 56 | 12 | 22 | 7 |
| Llanos | 46 | 11 | 23 | 8 | 36 | 7 | 20 | 8 | 40 | 6 | 15 | 5 |
| Western Ecuador moist forests | 45 | 14 | 31 | 11 | 33 | 6 | 16 | 9 | 56 | 8 | 14 | 4 |
| Magdalena/Urabá moist forests | 43 | 19 | 44 | 16 | 40 | 7 | 21 | 12 | 57 | 11 | 19 | 4 |
| Venezuelan Andes montane forests | 39 | 16 | 41 | 13 | 38 | 7 | 20 | 11 | 55 | 9 | 20 | 5 |
| Cauca Valley montane forests | 38 | 18 | 47 | 15 | 36 | 7 | 19 | 11 | 57 | 10 | 17 | 4 |
| Santa Marta montane forests | 38 | 21 | 55 | 17 | 38 | 10 | 15 | 11 | 73 | 9 | 15 | 6 |
| Magdalena Valley montane forests | 37 | 16 | 43 | 13 | 36 | 8 | 19 | 11 | 57 | 9 | 18 | 5 |
| Mangroves* | 33 | 7 | 21 | 5 | 20 | 3 | 6 | 4 | 66 | 3 | 3 | 2 |
| Guianan highlands moist forests | 32 | 13 | 40 | 11 | 30 | 6 | 22 | 11 | 50 | 10 | 20 | 4 |
| Japura/Negro moist forests | 32 | 14 | 43 | 11 | 30 | 7 | 21 | 12 | 57 | 10 | 19 | 6 |
| Varzea forests | 30 | 5 | 16 | 4 | 21 | 1 | 17 | 5 | 29 | 4 | 12 | 1 |
| Cauca Valley dry forests | 27 | 7 | 25 | 5 | 23 | 4 | 8 | 3 | 37 | 2 | 6 | 2 |
| Magdalena Valley dry forests | 27 | 8 | 29 | 5 | 25 | 6 | 9 | 5 | 55 | 3 | 8 | 4 |

| | | | | | | | | | | | |
|---|---|---|---|---|---|---|---|---|---|---|---|
| Maracaibo dry forests | 26 | 10 | 38 | 9 | 22 | 5 | 11 | 6 | 54 | 6 | 8 | 3 |
| Western Amazon swamp forests | 25 | 6 | 24 | 5 | 19 | 3 | 17 | 6 | 35 | 5 | 12 | 3 |
| Northern Andean paramo | 21 | 3 | 14 | 3 | 15 | 2 | 12 | 3 | 25 | 3 | 8 | 2 |
| Eastern Panamanian montane forests | 19 | 9 | 47 | 7 | 19 | 4 | 7 | 4 | 57 | 4 | 7 | 1 |
| Pelagic* | 14 | 5 | 35 | 4 | 4 | 2 | 6 | 3 | 50 | 2 | 3 | 2 |
| Patia dry forests | 12 | 4 | 33 | 2 | 11 | 3 | 5 | 3 | 60 | 2 | 4 | 2 |
| Santa Marta paramo | 12 | 4 | 33 | 4 | 11 | 3 | 7 | 4 | 57 | 4 | 7 | 3 |
| Macarena montane forests | 11 | 8 | 72 | 7 | 11 | 3 | 10 | 7 | 70 | 6 | 10 | 3 |
| Amazonian savannas | 7 | 2 | 28 | 2 | 5 | 0 | 7 | 2 | 28 | 2 | 5 | 0 |

[1] Species of conservation concern: Species with PIF concern scores that are >18 and/or statistically significant negative U.S. Breeding Bird Survey (BBS) population trends.

[2] Partners in Flight (PIF) concern scores that are greater than 18.

[3] Breeding Bird Survey U.S. trend, 1966-1991. Columns indicate number of birds with trends and declines that differ significantly from zero (p<.10).

[4] Ecoregions derived from the WB/WWF Conservation Assessment (Dinerstein et al. 1995).

* This ecoregion designation was created for this study and does not conform to WB/WWF dataset.

Table

3

# Figure 3.4  Ecoregions and Parks in Peril Sites of Colombia

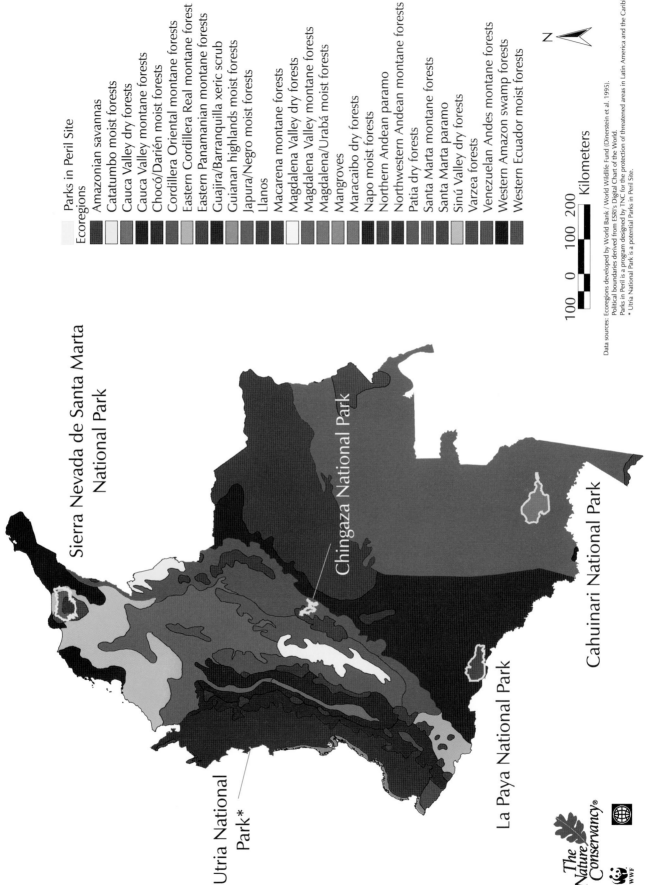

Sierra Nevada de Santa Marta National Park

Utria National Park*

Chingaza National Park

La Paya National Park

Cahuinari National Park

Parks in Peril Site

Ecoregions

Amazonian savannas
Catatumbo moist forests
Cauca Valley dry forests
Cauca Valley montane forests
Chocó/Darién moist forests
Cordillera Oriental montane forests
Eastern Cordillera Real montane forest
Eastern Panamanian montane forests
Guajira/Barranquilla xeric scrub
Guianan highlands moist forests
Japura/Negro moist forests
Llanos
Macarena montane forests
Magdalena Valley dry forests
Magdalena Valley montane forests
Magdalena/Urabá moist forests
Mangroves
Maracaibo dry forests
Napo moist forests
Northern Andean paramo
Northwestern Andean montane forests
Patia dry forests
Santa Marta montane forests
Santa Marta paramo
Sinú Valley dry forests
Varzea forests
Venezuelan Andes montane forests
Western Amazon swamp forests
Western Ecuador moist forests

N

100   0   100  200
Kilometers

Data sources: Ecoregions developed by World Bank / World Wildlife Fund (Dinerstein et al. 1995).
Political boundaries derived from ESRI's Digital Chart of the World.
Parks in Peril is a program designed by TNC for the protection of threatened areas in Latin America and the Caribbean.
* Utria National Park is a potential Parks in Peril Site.

The Nature Conservancy®

WWF

# Figure 3.5 Migrant Species Richness in Ecoregions of Colombia

## All Species

## Species with a South American Affinity

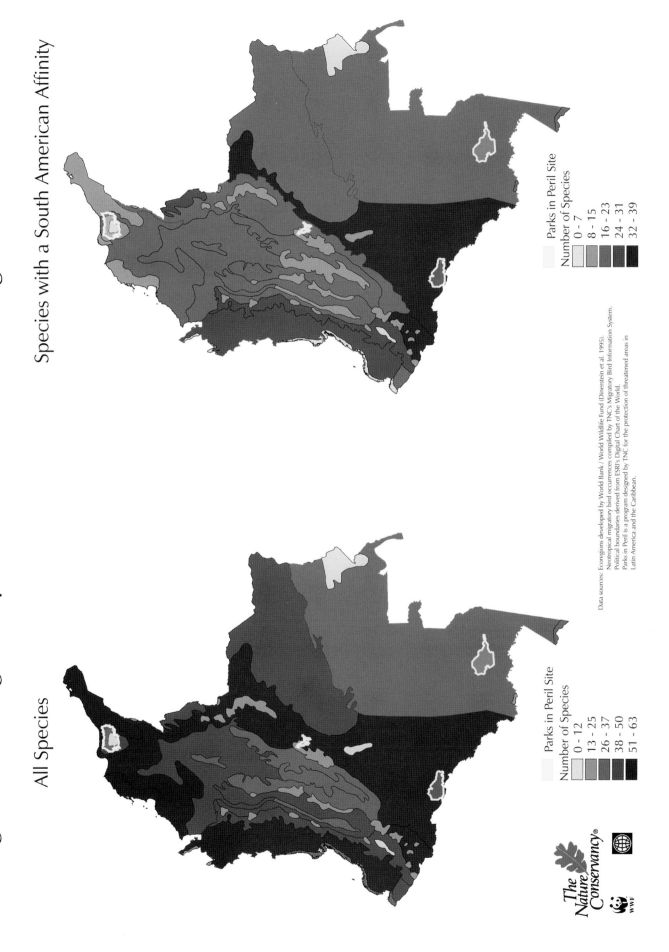

Data sources: Ecoregions developed by World Bank / World Wildlife Fund (Dinerstein et al. 1995).
Neotropical migratory bird occurrences compiled by TNC's Migratory Bird Information System.
Political boundaries derived from ESRI's Digital Chart of the World.
Parks in Peril is a program designed by TNC for the protection of threatened areas in
Latin America and the Caribbean.

# Figure 3.6  Migrant Species Richness in Ecoregions of Colombia:
## Species of Conservation Concern

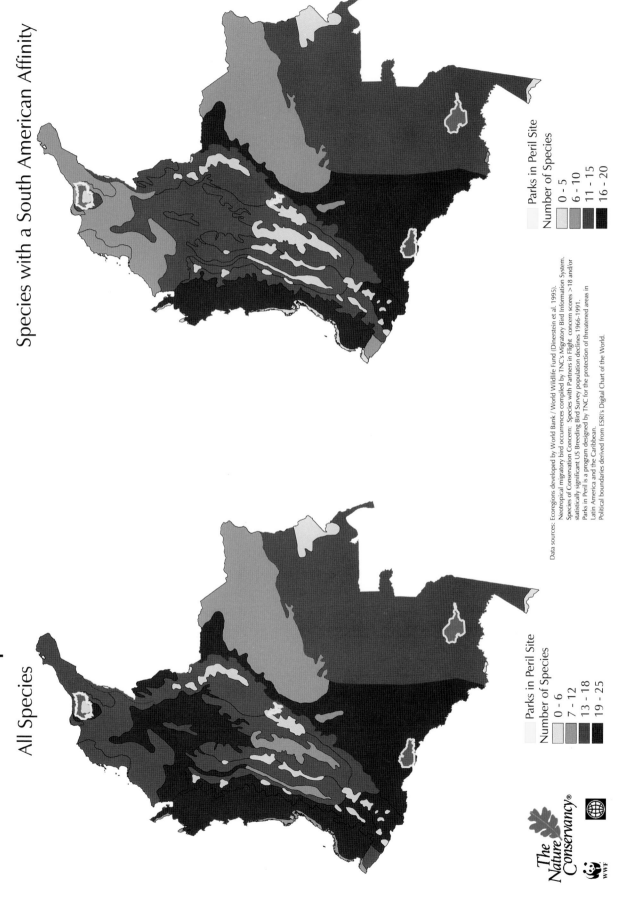

All Species

Species with a South American Affinity

Parks in Peril Site
Number of Species
0 - 6
7 - 12
13 - 18
19 - 25

Parks in Peril Site
Number of Species
0 - 5
6 - 10
11 - 15
16 - 20

Data sources: Ecoregions developed by World Bank / World Wildlife Fund (Dinerstein et al. 1995).
Neotropical migratory bird occurrences compiled by TNC's Migratory Bird Information System.
Species of Conservation Concern:  Species with Partners in Flight concern scores >18 and/or
statistically significant US Breeding Bird Survey population declines 1966-1991.
Parks in Peril is a program designed by TNC for the protection of threatened areas in
Latin America and the Caribbean.
Political boundaries derived from ESRI's Digital Chart of the World.

# Ecuador

Ecuador is a country of startling contrasts, ranging from snow-covered volcanoes to the Galapagos Islands, where penguins waddle through cactus forests. With these extraordinary landscapes, Ecuador has one of the highest biodiversity indexes per area of any on earth.[48] It also has a high degree of endemism for both plants and animals. More than 1,250 species of vascular plants have been recorded in less than 1 square kilometer, including 43 species endemic to a small area bordering the Rio Palenque. The country also has 307 species of vertebrates that are endemics.

This species-rich nation harbors 14 regional ecosystems including the lush Napo region, the montane and submontane forests of the Andes (which carve through the interior), the dry forests of the coast, the paramo, mangroves, and flooded grasslands. (See Figure 3.7.) Of the 14 ecoregions within Ecuador's boundaries, three are unique to Ecuador: the Ecuadorian dry forests, Galapagos Islands xeric scrub, and Guayaquil flooded grasslands. (See Figure 3.7.)

The Amazonian region of Ecuador still retains approximately half of its forests, but deforestation in the highlands is severe and remaining forest cover along the coast has been estimated to be only 6 percent.[49] There are 15 protected areas in Ecuador.[50]

More than 1,600 species of birds are found in Ecuador's 455,502 square kilometers.[51] Included in this area, which is roughly the size of Mississippi, are approximately 100 endemic species in the northern, southwestern, and central Andean regions. Offshore from Ecuador, the famous and pristine Galapagos Islands, immortalized by Charles Darwin, harbor a number of bird species. A full 75 percent of them are endemics.

Ninety-seven neotropical migrants occur in Ecuador as regular migrants. (See Tables 2.3 and 3.7.) The greatest species richness of neotropical migrants is found east of the Andes and on the coast. (See Table 3.3 and Figure 3.8.) In particular, the coastal Ecuadorian dry forests are known for high levels of regional and local endemism.[52] The counts are due not only to landbirds but also to the great number of shorebirds that fly to the coast of Ecuador.

The species-rich Napo forests[53] and the eastern Cordillera Real montane forests (exceptionally rich in species and containing a high proportion of regional and local endemics)[54] are also ecoregions with high migratory species richness. A small section of the Chocó/Darién moist forests is also species rich, but it should be noted that this ecoregion is mostly in Colombia with little overlap into Ecuador. (See Figure 3.4.) The number of migratory species recorded for the Galapagos Islands is relatively high.[55] However, most of the migrants use the islands irregularly, so the Galapagos are an important nonbreeding ground for only six migratory species.[56]

*The broad-winged hawk's future is uncertain. The Ecuadorian highlands, where deforestation is severe, is an important nonbreeding destination for this beautiful raptor, whose massive group migratory flights have given many a northern birdwatcher a once-in-a-lifetime experience.*

A great number of species with a South American affinity (47 species) occur in Ecuador. (See Tables 2.3 and 3.7.) The highest species richness of these birds generally is found in the Andes and east of the mountains, the Napo moist forests, and the eastern Cordillera Real montane forests. (See Table 3.3 and Figure 3.8.)

Ecuador is an important non breeding destination for the broad-winged hawk, a beautiful raptor with a South American affinity. For northern birdwatchers, the massive southward group flights of this raptor are a breathtaking sight. As many as 20,000 individual birds have passed a single point at any one time. The broad-winged

hawk comes from as far north as Canada to winter in the shelter that the Ecuadorian Andes provide. This hawk is particularly vulnerable to deforestation.

Ecuador has eight Parks in Peril sites (the most sites of any nation in the region), which represent seven ecoregions. (See Table 2.4 and Figure 3.7.) Of these ecoregions, the Galapagos Islands xeric scrub and Ecuadorian dry forests are unique to Ecuador.

In the montane cloud forests of the western slopes of the Andes is Maquipucuna Park, guardian of an abundance of wildlife and waters of critical importance to local people.[57] To the east, nestled in the Andes, is Cayambe-Coca Ecological Reserve, where the chilly paramo captures a rich source of water for the region.[58] South of Cayambe-Coca is Antisana Ecological Reserve, which protects a significant portion of Ecuador's biological diversity.[59]

East in the Amazonian lowlands is Yasuni National Park, classified as moist tropical forest yet also abundant in wetlands, marshes, and lakes. On the western coast is Machalilla National Park, the only marine park in continental Ecuador and preserver of one of the last remnants of coastal cloud forest.[60] In the Pacific are Galapagos Marine Reserve and Galapagos National Park, whose isolated natural histories have resulted in a fascinating endemism. The only park in southern Ecuador is Podocarpus National Park, which harbors the largest forests of native Andean conifers and several important watersheds.[61] Each of the eight Parks in Peril sites of Ecuador host at least 43 migratory species; one site has an estimated 62 species. (See Tables 2.4 and 3.7.)

Ecuador has 32 migrants of conservation concern. (See Tables 2.3 and 3.7.) Of these, 23 are species with a South American affinity. The Napo moist forests, eastern Cordillera Real montane forests, Ecuadorian dry forests, and the Chocó/Darién moist forests are the Ecuadorian ecoregions with the greatest species richness for the 32 species and the South American affinity subgroup. (See Figure 3.9.)

The futures of the broad-winged hawk, Swainson's hawk, American golden-plover, upland sandpiper, barn swallow, and yellow-green vireo are also uncertain. Conservation plans for Ecuador should take into account the habitat necessary to preserve these 29 species as well as other important biota.

# Table 3.3 Distribution and Conservation Status of Neotropical Migratory Birds in Ecuador

Species richness, number (and percent) of conservation concern (as indicated by high Partners in Flight concern scores and/or US Breeding Bird Survey population declines) for all migrants and for the subset of migrants with a South American Affinity are given. See footnotes for details.

| Ecoregions[4] | All Neotropical Migrants | | | | | Migrants with a South American Affinity | | | | |
|---|---|---|---|---|---|---|---|---|---|---|
| | Species | Cons. Concern[1] # | % | PIF[2] >18 | BBS Trends[3] # | Dec. | Species | Cons. Concern[1] # | % | PIF[2] >18 | BBS Trends[3] # | Dec. |

| Ecoregions[4] | Species | Cons. Concern # | % | PIF >18 | BBS # | Dec. | Species | Cons. Concern # | % | PIF >18 | BBS # | Dec. |
|---|---|---|---|---|---|---|---|---|---|---|---|---|
| Ecuadorian dry forests | 62 | 17 | 27 | 14 | 36 | 7 | 25 | 11 | 44 | 10 | 15 | 5 |
| Napo moist forests | 52 | 20 | 38 | 14 | 39 | 9 | 36 | 17 | 47 | 13 | 27 | 7 |
| Chocó/Darién moist forests | 49 | 19 | 38 | 15 | 38 | 8 | 25 | 14 | 56 | 12 | 20 | 6 |
| Eastern Cordillera Real montane forest | 49 | 18 | 36 | 13 | 41 | 9 | 32 | 16 | 50 | 13 | 26 | 7 |
| Galapagos Islands xeric scrub | 46 | 8 | 17 | 6 | 24 | 3 | 16 | 5 | 31 | 4 | 10 | 2 |
| Western Ecuador moist forests | 44 | 13 | 29 | 10 | 32 | 6 | 15 | 8 | 53 | 7 | 13 | 4 |
| Northwestern Andean montane forests | 43 | 15 | 34 | 12 | 37 | 7 | 23 | 12 | 52 | 11 | 20 | 5 |
| Mangroves* | 34 | 7 | 20 | 4 | 20 | 4 | 7 | 4 | 57 | 3 | 3 | 2 |
| Varzea forests | 30 | 5 | 16 | 4 | 21 | 1 | 17 | 5 | 29 | 4 | 12 | 1 |
| Guayaquil flooded grasslands | 29 | 5 | 17 | 3 | 18 | 2 | 6 | 3 | 50 | 2 | 4 | 1 |
| Tumbes/Piura dry forests | 26 | 6 | 23 | 4 | 16 | 4 | 7 | 3 | 42 | 3 | 7 | 2 |
| Northern Andean paramo | 20 | 2 | 10 | 2 | 14 | 2 | 11 | 2 | 18 | 2 | 7 | 2 |
| Pelagic* | 16 | 7 | 43 | 5 | 5 | 3 | 7 | 4 | 57 | 3 | 3 | 2 |
| Cordillera Central paramo | 11 | 2 | 18 | 2 | 8 | 2 | 8 | 2 | 25 | 2 | 5 | 2 |

[1] Species of conservation concern: Species with PIF concern scores that are >18 and/or statistically significant negative U.S. Breeding Bird Survey (BBS) population trends.

[2] Partners in Flight (PIF) concern scores that are greater than 18.

[3] Breeding Bird Survey U.S. trend, 1966-1991. Columns indicate number of birds with trends and declines that differ significantly from zero (p<.10).

[4] Ecoregions derived from the WB/WWF Conservation Assessment (Dinerstein et al. 1995).

* This ecoregion designation was created for this study and does not conform to WB/WWF dataset.

# Figure 3.7 Ecoregions and Parks in Peril Sites of Ecuador

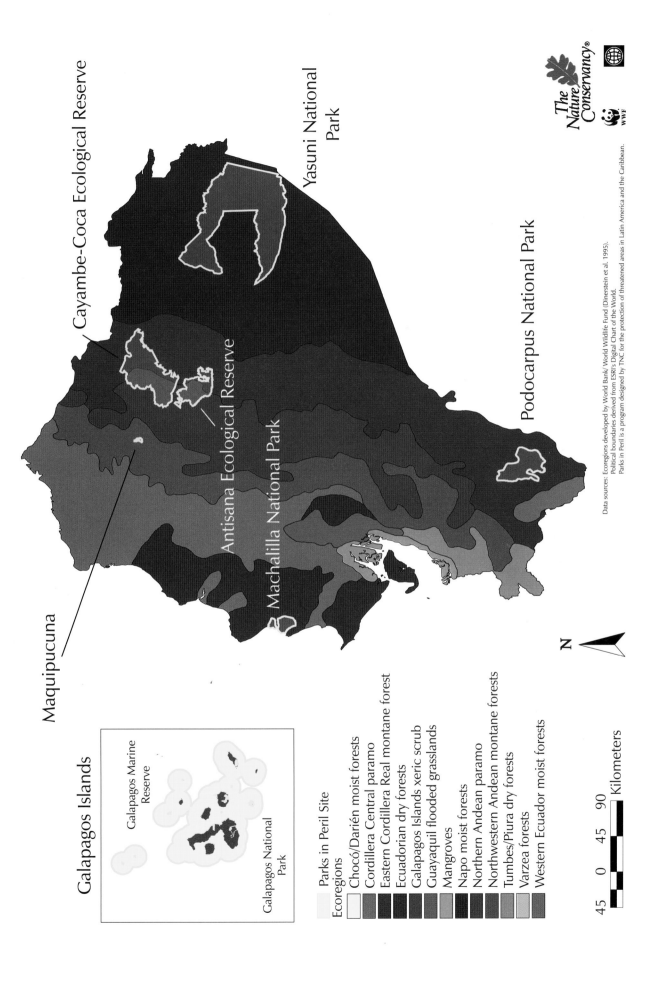

Cayambe-Coca Ecological Reserve

Yasuni National Park

Podocarpus National Park

Antisana Ecological Reserve

Machalilla National Park

Maquipucuna

Galapagos Islands

Galapagos Marine Reserve

Galapagos National Park

Parks in Peril Site
Ecoregions
Chocó/Darién moist forests
Cordillera Central paramo
Eastern Cordillera Real montane forest
Ecuadorian dry forests
Galapagos Islands xeric scrub
Guayaquil flooded grasslands
Mangroves
Napo moist forests
Northern Andean paramo
Northwestern Andean montane forests
Tumbes/Piura dry forests
Varzea forests
Western Ecuador moist forests

N

45  0  45  90
Kilometers

45  0

Data sources: Ecoregions developed by World Bank/ World Wildlife Fund (Dinerstein et al. 1995).
Political boundaries derived from ESRI's Digital Chart of the World.
Parks in Peril is a program designed by TNC for the protection of threatened areas in Latin America and the Caribbean.

The Nature Conservancy®

WWF

# Figure 3.8  Migrant Species Richness in Ecoregions of Ecuador

## All Species

## Species with a South American Affinity

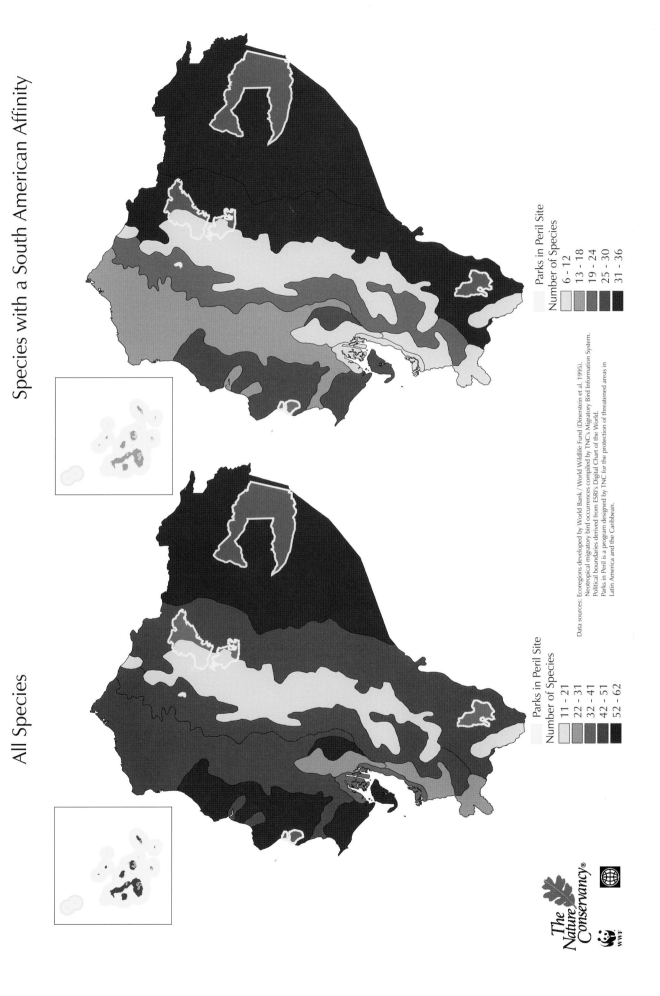

**Parks in Peril Site**

**Number of Species**
- 11 – 21
- 22 – 31
- 32 – 41
- 42 – 51
- 52 – 62

**Parks in Peril Site**

**Number of Species**
- 6 – 12
- 13 – 18
- 19 – 24
- 25 – 30
- 31 – 36

Data sources: Ecoregions developed by World Bank / World Wildlife Fund (Dinerstein et al. 1995).
Neotropical migratory bird occurrences compiled by TNC's Migratory Bird Information System.
Political boundaries derived from ESRI's Digital Chart of the World.
Parks in Peril is a program designed by TNC for the protection of threatened areas in
Latin America and the Caribbean.

# Figure 3.9  Migrant Species Richness in Ecoregions of Ecuador:
## Species of Conservation Concern

### All Species

### Species with a South American Affinity

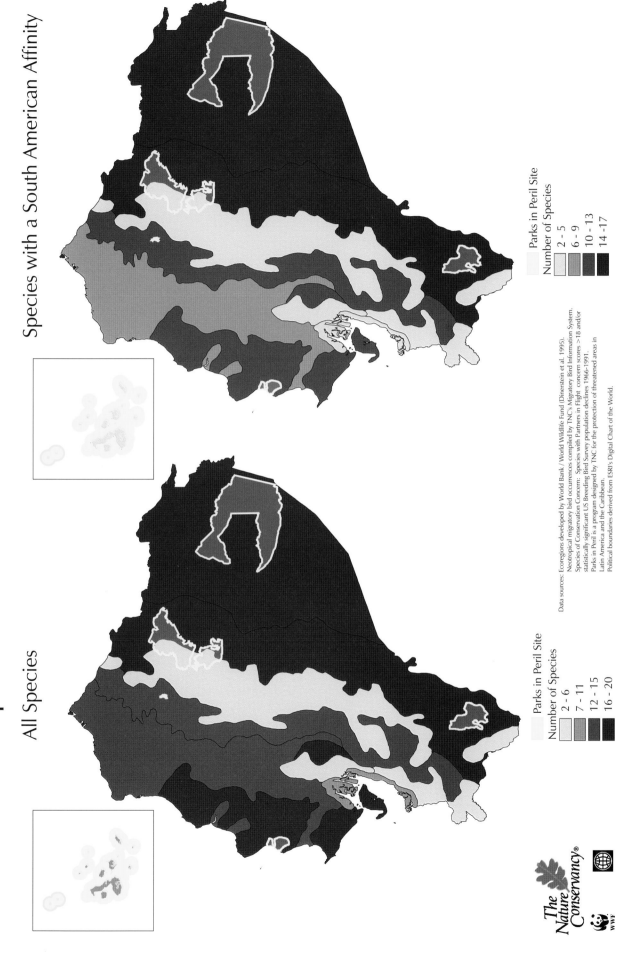

Parks in Peril Site

Number of Species
- 2 – 6
- 7 – 11
- 12 – 15
- 16 – 20

Parks in Peril Site

Number of Species
- 2 – 5
- 6 – 9
- 10 – 13
- 14 –17

Data sources: Ecoregions developed by World Bank / World Wildlife Fund (Dinerstein et al. 1995).
Neotropical migratory bird occurrences compiled by TNC's Migratory Bird Information System.
Species of Conservation Concern:  Species with Partners in Flight concern scores >18 and/or
statistically significant US Breeding Bird Survey population declines 1966-1991.
Parks in Peril is a program designed by TNC for the protection of threatened areas in
Latin America and the Caribbean.
Political boundaries derived from ESRI's Digital Chart of the World.

The Nature Conservancy®

WWF

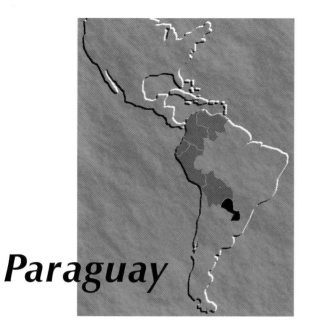

# Paraguay

Paraguay is the land of the wild chaco. These extensive and majestic open shrublands are home to the greater rhea, which is closely related to the African ostrich. Paraguay is the mother of many other endemic species as well, such as the bare-throated bellbird.

The wetlands that cover the chaco are important as they provide refuge to thousands of migratory waders in spring and autumn. Within Paraguay's 406,750 square kilometers, more than 650 bird species have been reliably recorded.[62] This is approximately the same as the number of birds that breed in North America, even though Paraguay is only 2.1 percent of its size.

In all, five ecoregions lie partially within Paraguay's national boundaries, being shared with bordering nations. (See Figure 3.10.) One of these ecoregions is a very special forest in the far eastern portion of the nation. The forest is exceptional because it is the last significant example of the "Alto Parana Formation" of the Atlantic forest, which has been almost entirely destroyed in neighboring Brazil. The interior Atlantic forests protect several imperiled endemic species.

Species richness is generally higher in the western half of the country, where the chaco savannas (which support a diverse flora and fauna with many regional endemics)[63] and the humid chaco ecoregions provide refuge for the greatest number of migratory species. (See Table 3.4 and Figure 3.11.) The remaining two ecoregions harbor similar species richness. The portion of pantanal that extends into Paraguay represents one of the world's largest wetland complexes and supports abundant populations of wildlife, and the cerrado is one of the largest savanna forest complexes in the world.[64]

Paraguay, together with northeastern Argentina, plays an important role in biodiversity conservation inasmuch it hosts a large number of threatened endemic plants and animals of the Atlantic forest.[65] Paraguay has 19 protected areas that preserve these rich biological resources.[66]

The Paraguay River courses through the middle of the nation, flowing from a number of smaller rivers and their watersheds. The waterway gives life to all living creatures in the area and acts as a highway for migratory birds.

Paraguay harbors 28 regularly reported neotropical migrants. (See Tables 2.3 and 3.7.) Because it is the southernmost of the six nations of the region, it is to be expected that fewer neotropical migrants fly as far as its boundaries. Of those species that do, however, it is notable that wading birds are well represented. This could be an indication that Paraguay's wetlands are significant to the waders or at least of enough importance for them to expend the greater energy required than if they were to finish their journeys farther north.

**In spring and autumn, the wetlands of Paraguay's wild chaco provide refuge to thousands of migratory waders such as the solitary sandpiper, one of the species with a South America affinity. That is to say, this incredibly tame migrant's main nonbreeding destination is South America.**

Twenty-two species with a South American affinity occur in Paraguay. (See Tables 2.4 and 3.7.) The ecoregions with the highest richness for these species are the chaco savannas and humid chaco. (See Figure 3.11.) The Brazilian interior Atlantic forests and pantanal ecoregions host comparable numbers of species with a South American affinity. (See Table 3.4.)

The numerous wetlands of the chaco of Paraguay provide nonbreeding habitat for the solitary sandpiper. This bird is a relatively common migrant in Paraguay, where it wades in shallow waters that provide it with sustenance in the form of insects and small crustaceans. This bird,

named for its tendency for being seen alone or in pairs and small groups, is tame and incredibly unwary of humans. It also is a species with a South American affinity.

One Parks in Peril site and one potential site (Defensores del Chaco National Park) are located in Paraguay. The sites represent two distinct ecoregions. Defensores del Chaco National Park is situated in the dry chaco of the north and consists of semideciduous dry forest that supports a diverse flora and fauna with many regional endemics. (See Table 2.3 and Figure 3.10.) To the east, the humid subtropical forests of the interior Atlantic forest of Mbaracayu Nature Reserve provide refuge to many plants and animals that were once found in the now largely destroyed Atlantic forest of Brazil.[67] Defensores del Chaco National Park and Mbaracayu Nature Reserve protect an estimated 27 and 24 species respectively. (See Tables 2.4 and 3.7.)

Of Paraguay's 28 migratory species, nine are of conservation concern. (See Tables 2.3 and 3.7.) All of these are neotropical migrants with a South American affinity. The ecoregions with the highest richness for these species are the chaco savannas, humid chaco, and Brazilian interior Atlantic forests. (See Table 3.4 and Figure 3.12.)

Particular uncertainty also exists over the future of the Swainson's hawk, American golden-plover, upland sandpiper, and barn swallow, all species that occur in Paraguay. These 13 species should be given priority, along with other important biota, when designing conservation plans for Paraguay.

## Table 3.4 *Distribution and Conservation Status of Neotropical Migratory Birds in Paraguay*

Species richness, number (and percent) of conservation concern (as indicated by high Partners in Flight concern scores and/or US Breeding Bird Survey population declines) for all migrants and for the subset of migrants with a South American Affinity are given. See footnotes for details.

| Ecoregions[4] | All Neotropical Migrants | | | | | | Migrants with a South American Affinity | | | | | |
|---|---|---|---|---|---|---|---|---|---|---|---|---|
| | Species | Cons. Concern[1] # | % | PIF[2] >18 | BBS Trends[3] # | Dec. | Species | Cons. Concern[1] # | % | PIF[2] >18 | BBS Trends[3] # | Dec. |
| Humid Chaco | 27 | 8 | 29 | 7 | 18 | 2 | 21 | 8 | 38 | 7 | 13 | 2 |
| Chaco savannas | 27 | 8 | 29 | 7 | 18 | 2 | 21 | 8 | 38 | 7 | 13 | 2 |
| Pantanal | 24 | 6 | 25 | 5 | 16 | 2 | 19 | 6 | 31 | 5 | 12 | 2 |
| Brazilian Interior Atlantic forests | 24 | 7 | 29 | 6 | 17 | 2 | 19 | 7 | 36 | 6 | 14 | 2 |
| Cerrado | 21 | 5 | 23 | 4 | 17 | 2 | 15 | 5 | 33 | 4 | 12 | 2 |

[1] Species of conservation concern: Species with PIF concern scores that are >18 and/or statistically significant negative U.S. Breeding Bird Survey (BBS) population trends.
[2] Partners in Flight (PIF) concern scores that are greater than 18.
[3] Breeding Bird Survey U.S. trend, 1966-1991. Columns indicate number of birds with trends and declines that differ significantly from zero (p<.10).
[4] Ecoregions derived from the WB/WWF Conservation Assessment (Dinerstein et al. 1995).

# Figure 3.10 Ecoregions and Parks in Peril Sites of Paraguay

Defensores del Chaco National Park*

Parks in Peril Site

Ecoregions

Brazilian Interior Atlantic Forest
Cerrado
Chaco savannas
Humid Chaco
Pantanal

Mbaracayu Nature Reserve

N

41   0   41   82
Kilometers

Data sources: Ecoregions developed by World Bank / World Wildlife Fund (Dinerstein et al. 1995).
Political boundaries derived from ESRI's Digital Chart of the World.
Parks in Peril is a program designed by TNC for the protection of threatened areas in Latin America and the Caribbean.
* Defensores del Chaco National Park is a potential Parks in Peril Site.

The Nature Conservancy®

WWF

# Figure 3.11 Migrant Species Richness in Ecoregions of Paraguay

## All Species

## Species with a South American Affinity

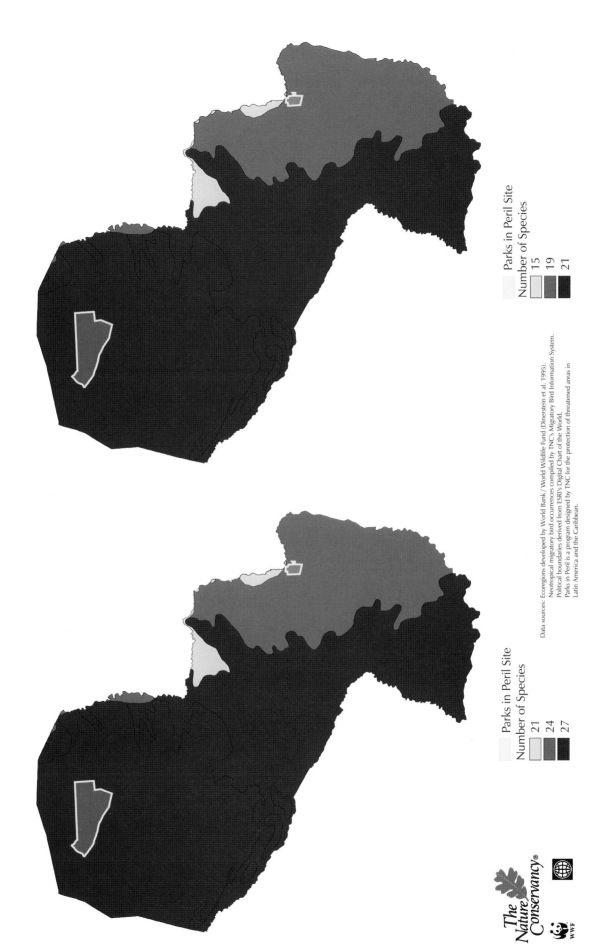

Parks in Peril Site
Number of Species
21
24
27

Parks in Peril Site
Number of Species
15
19
21

Data sources: Ecoregions developed by World Bank / World Wildlife Fund (Dinerstein et al. 1995).
Neotropical migratory bird occurrences compiled by TNC's Migratory Bird Information System.
Political boundaries derived from ESRI's Digital Chart of the World.
Parks in Peril is a program designed by TNC for the protection of threatened areas in Latin America and the Caribbean.

# Figure 3.12   Migrant Species Richness in Ecoregions of Paraguay: Species of Conservation Concern

## All Species

## Species with a South American Affinity

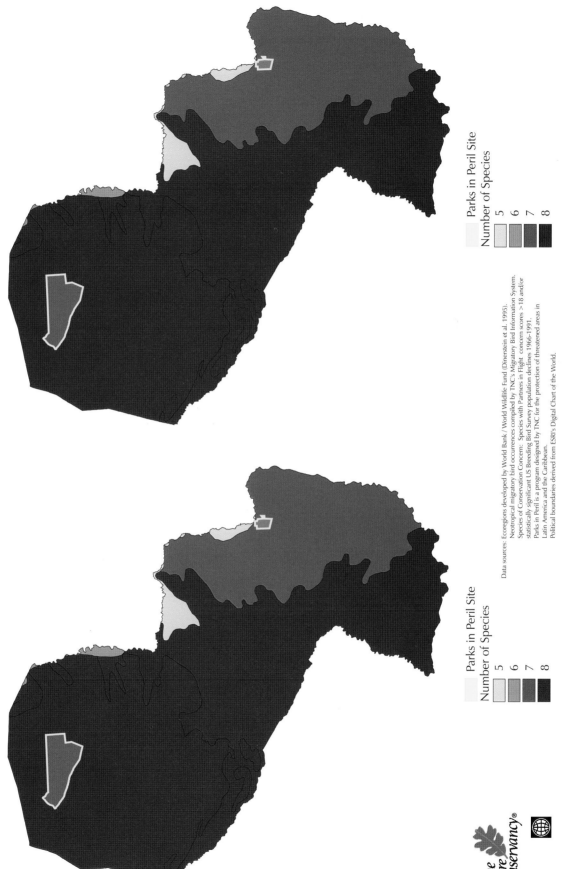

Parks in Peril Site
Number of Species
5
6
7
8

Parks in Peril Site
Number of Species
5
6
7
8

Data sources: Ecoregions developed by World Bank / World Wildlife Fund (Dinerstein et al. 1995).
Neotropical migratory bird occurrences compiled by TNC's Migratory Bird Information System.
Species of Conservation Concern: Species with Partners in Flight concern scores >18 and/or
statistically significant US Breeding Bird Survey population declines 1966-1991.
Parks in Peril is a program designed by TNC for the protection of threatened areas in
Latin America and the Caribbean.
Political boundaries derived from ESRI's Digital Chart of the World.

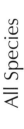

# Peru

Peru is a nation of great contrasts. A bird flying from west to east would see sparkling desert, majestic mountains, wide paramos, and eventually the lush green forest of the Amazon. It might fly over the varzea's seasonally flooded forests or the puna grasslands of the High Andes. The mountains extend through the entire central and eastern portions of the country, and they support the most diverse vegetation on the planet. Lake Titicaca, the highest navigable lake in the world, lies cradled in the Andes along the Bolivian border.

This nation of such extremes is a haven to wildlife. Its 1,285,215 square kilometers contain 460 species of mammals, 365 species of reptiles, and 315 species of amphibians.[68] The famous and mysterious Andean condor soars over the paramos, the freshwater dolphin that has inspired romantic Peruvian legends swims peacefully in the rivers of the Amazon, while 31 species of monkeys and tamarins glide through the trees. Peru has 22 protected areas to perpetuate this bountiful biological diversity.[69]

Peru is also rich in birdlife. One national park, Manu, located in the forests of eastern Peru, harbors 1,000 species of birds. In fact, more than 20 percent of the world's birds—1,703 species[70]—are found in Peru, a nation only approximately twice the size of Texas.

No fewer than 84 migratory species occur as regular migrants. (See Tables 2.3 and 3.7.) Found within the country's borders are 20 ecoregions, two of which are unique to Peru: the Peruvian yungas and the Marañón dry forests. (See Figure 3.13.) The greatest species richness is generally found along the coast, in the eastern Andes, and in the Amazonian lowlands. (See Table 3.5 and Figure 3.14.) The highest species richness is found in the Sechura desert ecoregion, in large part due to the great number of shorebirds that flock to its beaches.

Another area with a high number of species is the Napo moist forests, noted to have the richest overall diversity of any area in South America. The eastern Cordillera Real montane forests (exceptionally rich in species and exhibiting a high proportion of regional and local endemics)[71] and the southwestern Amazonia moist forests are also ecoregions with high species richness.

Forty-six migrants with a South American affinity occur in Peru. (See Tables 2.3 and 3.7.) The ecoregions hosting the greatest number of these species are in Peru's elongated central section: again the Napo moist forests, eastern Cordillera Real montane forests, and the southwestern Amazonia moist forests. (See Table 3.5 and Figure 3.14.)

One regular and numerous visitor to Peru's Pacific coast is the black-bellied plover. This bird is the largest American plover, and in Peru it can be seen in coastal wetlands near river mouths and lagoons. It

© Amos Eno

*The black-bellied plover can be seen in Peru's coastal wetlands, including river mouths and lagoons. It is quick to give an alarm call at any sign of danger—vigilance that has saved it from the hunting pressures that threaten other species.*

is one of the many aquatic bird species that winter along Peru's coastline. The plover plays the role of sentinel for any shorebirds assembled nearby, being quick to give an alarm call at any sign of danger. This vigilance has resulted in the black-bellied plover's being unscathed by hunting pressures, unlike other species.

Four Parks in Peril sites and one potential site (Paracas) are found in Peru and overlay 10 ecoregions. (See Table 2.4 and Figure 3.13.) One of these ecoregions, the Peruvian yungas, is unique to Peru. To the northwest is Tabaconas Namballe National Sanctuary, nestled in the moist yungas. Another site, Pacaya-Samiria National

Reserve, is notable for the varzea forests, among the world's most extensive seasonally inundated forests. These forests support outstanding seasonal migrations of fish and mammals.[72]

Directly south, on the eastern slopes of the central forest of Peru, is Yanachaga-Chemillén National Park, which protects habitats with extremely variable altitudes. To the southeast is Pampas del Heath National Sanctuary with its extensive natural savanna, which harbors the only populations of many rare or endemic animals.[73] On the coast is Paracas National Reserve, a site with amazing congregations of shorebirds. All five sites host at least 39 migratory species each; one site harbors 54 species. (See Tables 2.4 and 3.7.)

Peru provides nonbreeding habitat for 29 migrants of conservation concern, 23 of which are species with a South American affinity. (See Tables 2.3 and 3.7.) The 23 species of conservation concern represent half of the total species with a South American affinity that occur in Peru.

The ecoregions with highest species richness for both the group of conservation concern and the subset with a South American affinity are the Napo moist forests, eastern Cordillera Real montane forests, and the southwestern Amazonia moist forests. (See Table 3.5 and Figure 3.15.) The Sechura desert is also high in species richness for the group of 29 migrants.

Peru provides nonbreeding homes for the broad-winged hawk, Swainson's hawk, American golden-plover, upland sandpiper, barn swallow, and yellow-green vireo. As noted in Chapter 2, the populations of these species have been flagged as precarious. A comprehensive conservation plan for Peru that includes the protection needs of these six species, along with the 23 above-mentioned species, will further the conservation of neotropical migratory birds.

## Table 3.5  Distribution and Conservation Status of Neotropical Migratory Birds in Peru

Species richness, number (and percent) of conservation concern (as indicated by high Partners in Flight concern scores and/or US Breeding Bird Survey population declines) for all migrants and for the subset of migrants with a South American Affinity are given. See footnotes for details.

| Ecoregions[4] | All Neotropical Migrants | | | | | | Migrants with a South American Affinity | | | | | |
| | Species | Cons. Concern[1] # | % | PIF[2] >18 # | BBS Trends[3] # | Dec. | Species | Cons. Concern[1] # | % | PIF[2] >18 # | BBS Trends[3] # | Dec. |
| --- | --- | --- | --- | --- | --- | --- | --- | --- | --- | --- | --- | --- | --- |
| Sechura desert | 54 | 14 | 25 | 10 | 26 | 5 | 23 | 9 | 39 | 7 | 13 | 3 |
| Napo moist forests | 47 | 19 | 40 | 13 | 35 | 9 | 35 | 17 | 48 | 13 | 26 | 7 |
| Eastern Cordillera Real montane forest | 44 | 17 | 38 | 12 | 36 | 9 | 30 | 15 | 50 | 12 | 24 | 7 |
| Southwestern Amazonia moist forests | 40 | 14 | 35 | 12 | 29 | 5 | 30 | 13 | 43 | 12 | 22 | 4 |
| Bolivian Yungas | 30 | 9 | 30 | 7 | 23 | 5 | 22 | 9 | 40 | 7 | 17 | 5 |
| Varzea forests | 30 | 5 | 16 | 4 | 21 | 1 | 17 | 5 | 29 | 4 | 12 | 1 |
| Peruvian Yungas | 29 | 13 | 44 | 9 | 26 | 8 | 18 | 11 | 61 | 9 | 16 | 6 |
| Western Amazon flooded grasslands | 28 | 5 | 17 | 4 | 21 | 2 | 19 | 5 | 26 | 4 | 13 | 2 |
| Ucayali moist forests | 27 | 12 | 44 | 10 | 23 | 6 | 21 | 11 | 52 | 10 | 17 | 5 |
| Japura/Negro moist forests | 26 | 10 | 38 | 7 | 24 | 6 | 18 | 9 | 50 | 7 | 16 | 5 |
| Tumbes/Piura dry forests | 26 | 6 | 23 | 4 | 16 | 4 | 7 | 3 | 42 | 3 | 7 | 2 |
| Western Amazon swamp forests | 25 | 6 | 24 | 5 | 19 | 3 | 17 | 6 | 35 | 5 | 12 | 3 |
| Central Andean wet puna | 21 | 5 | 23 | 4 | 12 | 2 | 11 | 4 | 36 | 3 | 6 | 2 |
| Mangroves* | 20 | 2 | 10 | 1 | 10 | 1 | 2 | 1 | 50 | 1 | 0 | 0 |
| Central Andean dry puna | 17 | 2 | 11 | 1 | 11 | 1 | 9 | 2 | 22 | 1 | 5 | 1 |
| Central Andean puna | 16 | 2 | 12 | 2 | 10 | 0 | 9 | 2 | 22 | 2 | 5 | 0 |

**Table 3.5** Distribution and Conservation Status of Neotropical Migratory Birds in Peru *(continued)*

| Ecoregions[4] | All Neotropical Migrants | | | | | Migrants with a South American Affinity | | | | |
| | Species | Cons. Concern[1] # | Cons. Concern[1] % | PIF[2] >18 | BBS Trends[3] # Dec. | Species | Cons. Concern[1] # | Cons. Concern[1] % | PIF[2] >18 | BBS Trends[3] # Dec. |
|---|---|---|---|---|---|---|---|---|---|---|
| Juruá moist forests | 13 | 5 | 38 | 4 | 11  3 | 11 | 5 | 45 | 4 | 10  3 |
| Pelagic* | 13 | 6 | 46 | 4 | 5  3 | 6 | 4 | 66 | 3 | 3  2 |
| Cordillera Central paramo | 11 | 2 | 18 | 2 | 8  2 | 8 | 2 | 25 | 2 | 5  2 |
| Marañón dry forests | 4 | 3 | 75 | 1 | 4  2 | 2 | 2 | 100 | 1 | 2  1 |

[1] Species of conservation concern: Species with PIF concern scores that are >18 and/or statistically significant negative U.S. Breeding Bird Survey (BBS) population trends.

[2] Partners in Flight (PIF) concern scores that are greater than 18.

[3] Breeding Bird Survey U.S. trend, 1966-1991. Columns indicate number of birds with trends and declines that differ significantly from zero (p<.10).

[4] Ecoregions derived from the WB/WWF Conservation Assessment (Dinerstein et al. 1995).

* This ecoregion designation was created for this study and does not conform to WB/WWF dataset.

Table

3

109

# Table 3.13  Ecoregions and Parks in Peril Sites in Peru

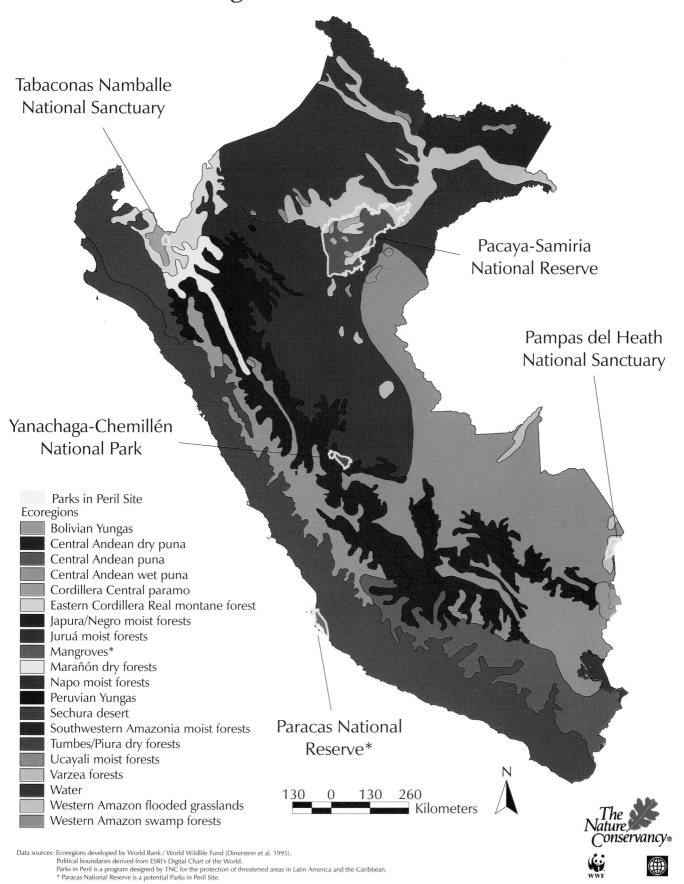

Tabaconas Namballe
National Sanctuary

Pacaya-Samiria
National Reserve

Pampas del Heath
National Sanctuary

Yanachaga-Chemillén
National Park

Paracas National
Reserve*

**Parks in Peril Site**

**Ecoregions**
- Bolivian Yungas
- Central Andean dry puna
- Central Andean puna
- Central Andean wet puna
- Cordillera Central paramo
- Eastern Cordillera Real montane forest
- Japura/Negro moist forests
- Juruá moist forests
- Mangroves*
- Marañón dry forests
- Napo moist forests
- Peruvian Yungas
- Sechura desert
- Southwestern Amazonia moist forests
- Tumbes/Piura dry forests
- Ucayali moist forests
- Varzea forests
- Water
- Western Amazon flooded grasslands
- Western Amazon swamp forests

130    0    130    260
Kilometers

N

*The Nature Conservancy®*

Data sources: Ecoregions developed by World Bank / World Wildlife Fund (Dinerstein et al. 1995).
   Political boundaries derived from ESRI's Digital Chart of the World.
   Parks in Peril is a program designed by TNC for the protection of threatened areas in Latin America and the Caribbean.
   * Paracas National Reserve is a potential Parks in Peril Site.

WWF

# Figure 3.14  Migrant Species Richness in Ecoregions of Peru

### Species with a South American Affinity

### All Species

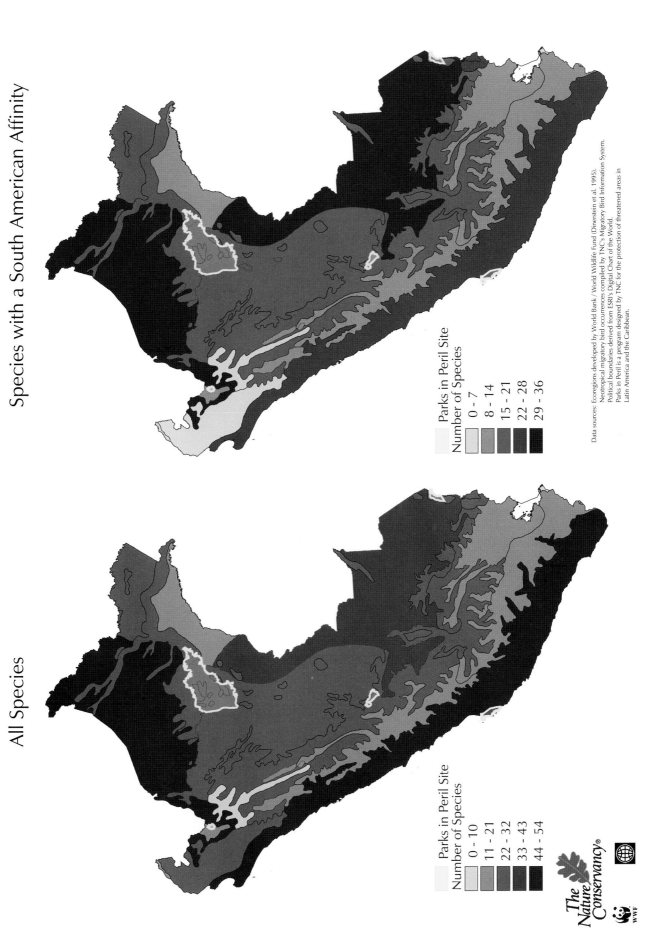

**Parks in Peril Site**
**Number of Species**
- 0 - 7
- 8 - 14
- 15 - 21
- 22 - 28
- 29 - 36

**Parks in Peril Site**
**Number of Species**
- 0 - 10
- 11 - 21
- 22 - 32
- 33 - 43
- 44 - 54

Data sources: Ecoregions developed by World Bank / World Wildlife Fund (Dinerstein et al. 1995).
Neotropical migratory bird occurrences compiled by TNC's Migratory Bird Information System.
Political boundaries derived from ESRI's Digital Chart of the World.
Parks in Peril is a program designed by TNC for the protection of threatened areas in
Latin America and the Caribbean.

# Figure 3.15   Migrant Species Richness in Ecoregions of Peru: Species of Conservation Concern

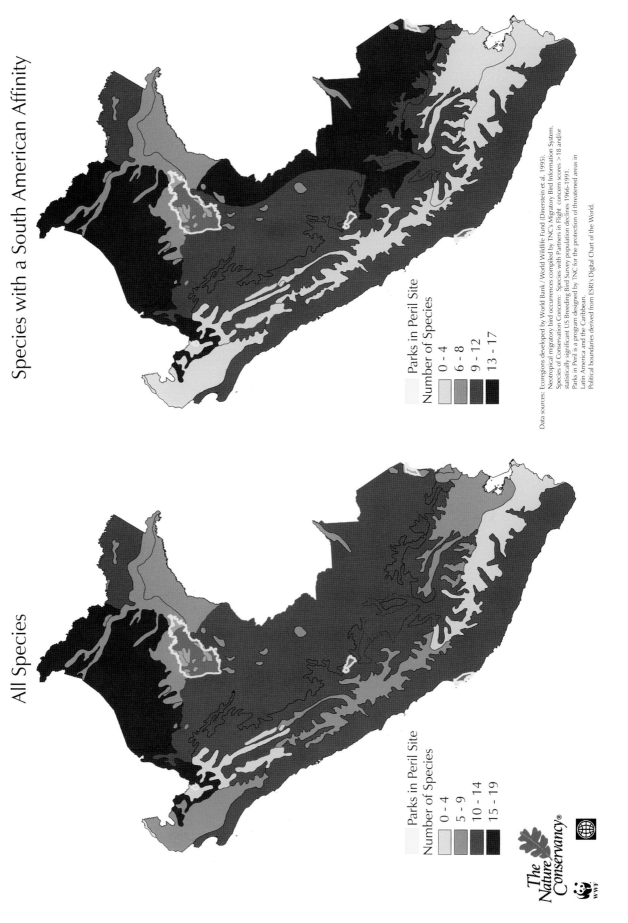

Species with a South American Affinity

Parks in Peril Site
Number of Species
0 - 4
6 - 8
9 - 12
13 - 17

All Species

Parks in Peril Site
Number of Species
0 - 4
5 - 9
10 - 14
15 - 19

Data sources: Ecoregions developed by World Bank / World Wildlife Fund (Dinerstein et al. 1995).
Neotropical migratory bird occurrences compiled by TNC's Migratory Bird Information System.
Species of Conservation Concern:  Species with Partners in Flight  concern scores >18 and/or
statistically significant US Breeding Bird Survey population declines 1966-1991.
Parks in Peril is a program designed by TNC for the protection of threatened areas in
Latin America and the Caribbean.
Political boundaries derived from ESRI's Digital Chart of the World.

The Nature Conservancy®

WWF

# Venezuela

The most spectacular and oldest geological formations in South America are Venezuela's remote Tepuis table-top mountains, which rise thousands of feet above the tropical jungle. Approximately 2.5 billion years ago, the entire area was a massive deposit of limestone as much as 10,000 feet thick. When this enormous limestone plateau eroded away, it left behind the Tepuis, which tower above the moist forests of the Guianan highlands in Venezuela's Pantepui region. In these mountains it is possible to find a new species in as little as 20 minutes of searching.

Another striking feature of the Venezuelan landscape is the 1,500-mile-long Orinoco River. The name means "father of our land," according to indigenous people. The Orinoco is one of hundreds of rivers that cross the country.

Venezuela harbors an impressive array of habitats in a relatively small area. In its 912,000 square kilometers are ecological regions such as the Andes, montane and submontane forests, dry forests, xeric habitats, coastal mountain range forests, mangroves, islands, Amazonian lowlands, the fabulous llanos, Orinoco Delta, paramos, and the unique Pantepui region. (See Figure 3.16.)

Venezuelan biodiversity is extremely rich. In addition to 2,600 species of orchids, Venezuela hosts more than 40 percent (1,323 species)[74] of all bird species found in South America. To preserve its varied biodiversity, Venezuela boasts 100 protected areas.[75]

With its varied habitats and strategic location along migration routes, Venezuela harbors important nonbreeding grounds for neotropical migratory birds. Venezuelan ecosystems are visited by 111 species of neotropical migrants. Additional migratory species arrive from the West Indies, a few fly up from southern South America, and others are transoceanic species migrating from higher Atlantic latitudes. (See Tables 2.3 and 3.7.)

Twenty-seven ecoregions are represented in Venezuela, and nine of them are unique to the nation. (See Figure 3.16.) Among them are the Cordillera de la Costa forests, Lara/Falcón dry forests, and the Orinoco wetlands. The ecoregions most frequented by migrants are mostly those in the north-central area. (See Table 3.6 and Figure 3.17.) The Cordillera de la Costa forests harbor the most species of migrants and have large numbers of regional and local endemics.[76] Other ecoregions with high species richness are the Guajira/Barranquilla xeric scrub, the Venezuelan islands,[77] and the La Costa xeric shrublands.

Forty-five species with a South American affinity occur in Venezuela. (See Tables 2.3 and 3.7.) The ecoregions with a high number of these species are the Napo moist forests, Cordillera de la Costa forests, and the Catatumbo moist forests. (See Table 3.6 and Figure 3.17.)

**The vast llanos of Venezuela form part of the main nonbreeding ground of the dickcissel, named for the territorial call the male makes upon arrival at its northern breeding grounds. The dickcissel feeds on rice and other seeds that make it vulnerable to pesticide poisoning.**

The vast llanos of Venezuela provide ideal nonbreeding habitat and also are part of the main wintering ground of the dickcissel. This charismatic, sparrow-like bird is named for the territorial call the male makes upon arrival at its northern breeding grounds. In Venezuela, its nonbreeding grounds are generally north of the Orinoco, and it arrives there in small groups as well as large flocks of 1,000 or more.[78] The bird uses open habitats and feeds on rice and other seeds that make it vulnerable to pesticide poisoning. Sadly, the dickcissel is of high conservation concern.

The two Parks in Peril sites in Venezuela represent five ecoregions. (See Table 2.4 and Figure 3.16.) Aguaro/Guariquito is situated in the llanos, which is the largest savanna ecosystem in northern South America.[79] The llanos is well known for its amazing concentrations of waterbirds.[80] To the east lies Canaima National Park, located amid the dramatic Tepuis and Guianan highlands, a region recognized as an evolutionary center for plant taxa found in Amazonia and the Guianan lowlands.[81] Canaima National Park provides refuge to an estimated 62 migratory species, and Aguaro/Guariquito shelters 46 species. (See Tables 2.4 and 3.7.)

Of the migrants that occur in Venezuela, 40 species are of conservation concern. (See Tables 2.3 and 3.7.) Twenty-five species, more than half of the 45 birds with a South American affinity that occur in Venezuela, are in this group of conservation concern. The highest species richness for the group of migrants of conservation concern as well as the subgroup can be found in the Cordillera de la Costa forests, Napo moist forests, and the Catatumbo moist forests. (See Table 3.6 and Figure 3.18.)

The broad-winged hawk, Swainson's hawk, American golden-plover, upland sandpiper, barn swallow, and yellow-green vireo are additional species that should be of concern to conservationists in Venezuela. The country is thus an important nonbreeding home for a total of 31 species of neotropical migrants with uncertain futures. The long-term prognosis for these species will improve if their habitat requirements are considered when designing conservation plans for Venezuela.

## Table 3.6 Distribution and Conservation Status of Neotropical Migratory Birds in Venezuela

Species richness, number (and percent) of conservation concern (as indicated by high Partners in Flight concern scores and/or US Breeding Bird Survey population declines) for all migrants and for the subset of migrants with a South American Affinity are given. See footnotes for details.

| Ecoregions[4] | All Neotropical Migrants | | | | | | Migrants with a South American Affinity | | | | | |
| | Species | Cons. Concern[1] # | % | PIF[2] >18 | BBS Trends[3] # | Dec. | Species | Cons. Concern[1] # | % | PIF[2] >18 | BBS Trends[3] # | Dec. |
|---|---|---|---|---|---|---|---|---|---|---|---|---|
| Cordillera de La Costa forests | 65 | 28 | 43 | 22 | 54 | 13 | 26 | 17 | 65 | 14 | 21 | 8 |
| Venezuelan Islands* | 59 | 23 | 38 | 17 | 52 | 11 | 25 | 14 | 56 | 11 | 24 | 8 |
| Guajira/Barranquilla xeric scrub | 59 | 14 | 23 | 12 | 39 | 6 | 14 | 7 | 50 | 6 | 8 | 4 |
| La Costa xeric shrublands | 57 | 17 | 29 | 11 | 44 | 8 | 18 | 10 | 55 | 7 | 14 | 5 |
| Napo moist forests | 55 | 22 | 40 | 16 | 42 | 11 | 37 | 18 | 48 | 14 | 28 | 8 |
| Cordillera Oriental montane forests | 50 | 17 | 34 | 14 | 48 | 9 | 22 | 10 | 45 | 7 | 21 | 6 |
| Catatumbo moist forests | 47 | 22 | 46 | 19 | 42 | 10 | 25 | 14 | 56 | 12 | 22 | 7 |
| Llanos | 46 | 11 | 23 | 8 | 36 | 7 | 20 | 8 | 40 | 6 | 16 | 5 |
| Venezuelan Andes montane forests | 39 | 16 | 41 | 13 | 38 | 7 | 20 | 11 | 55 | 9 | 20 | 5 |
| Mangroves* | 38 | 7 | 18 | 5 | 26 | 3 | 10 | 4 | 40 | 3 | 7 | 2 |
| Paraguaná xeric scrub | 36 | 10 | 27 | 9 | 26 | 4 | 7 | 4 | 57 | 4 | 7 | 2 |
| Lara/Falcón dry forests | 36 | 8 | 22 | 7 | 26 | 4 | 8 | 3 | 37 | 3 | 7 | 2 |
| Japura/Negro moist forests | 32 | 14 | 43 | 11 | 30 | 7 | 21 | 12 | 57 | 10 | 19 | 6 |
| Guianan highlands moist forests | 32 | 13 | 40 | 11 | 30 | 6 | 22 | 11 | 50 | 10 | 20 | 4 |
| Orinoco Delta swamp forests | 29 | 7 | 24 | 5 | 21 | 4 | 10 | 6 | 60 | 5 | 8 | 3 |
| Araya and Paría xeric scrub | 28 | 8 | 28 | 4 | 21 | 6 | 5 | 4 | 80 | 3 | 4 | 3 |
| Maracaibo dry forests | 25 | 10 | 40 | 9 | 21 | 5 | 11 | 6 | 54 | 6 | 8 | 3 |
| Northern Andean paramo | 19 | 3 | 15 | 3 | 13 | 2 | 11 | 3 | 27 | 3 | 7 | 2 |
| Cordillera de Mérida paramo | 17 | 3 | 17 | 3 | 12 | 1 | 11 | 3 | 27 | 3 | 7 | 1 |

**Table 3.6** *Distribution and Conservation Status of Neotropical Migratory Birds in Venezuela (continued)*

| | All Neotropical Migrants | | | | | | Migrants with a South American Affinity | | | | | |
| Ecoregions[4] | Species | Cons. Concern[1] # | % | PIF[2] >18 | BBS Trends[3] # | Dec. | Species | Cons. Concern[1] # | % | PIF[2] >18 | BBS Trends[3] # | Dec. |
|---|---|---|---|---|---|---|---|---|---|---|---|---|
| Orinoco wetlands | 14 | 3 | 21 | 2 | 11 | 1 | 4 | 3 | 75 | 2 | 3 | 1 |
| Guianan savannas | 14 | 4 | 28 | 3 | 11 | 2 | 11 | 4 | 36 | 3 | 9 | 2 |
| Tepuis | 13 | 6 | 46 | 5 | 13 | 2 | 10 | 5 | 50 | 5 | 10 | 1 |
| Llanos dry forests | 11 | 6 | 54 | 5 | 10 | 4 | 5 | 4 | 80 | 4 | 5 | 2 |
| Paraguaná restingas | 9 | 2 | 22 | 2 | 4 | 1 | 1 | 1 | 100 | 1 | 1 | 1 |
| Pelagic* | 7 | 3 | 42 | 1 | 3 | 2 | 2 | 2 | 100 | 1 | 2 | 1 |
| Amazonian savannas | 7 | 2 | 28 | 2 | 5 | 0 | 7 | 2 | 28 | 2 | 5 | 0 |
| Guianan moist forests | 4 | 2 | 50 | 1 | 4 | 1 | 4 | 2 | 50 | 1 | 4 | 1 |

[1] Species of conservation concern: Species with PIF concern scores that are >18 and/or statistically significant negative U.S. Breeding Bird Survey (BBS) population trends.

[2] Partners in Flight (PIF) concern scores that are greater than 18.

[3] Breeding Bird Survey U.S. trend, 1966-1991. Columns indicate number of birds with trends and declines that differ significantly from zero (p<.10).

[4] Ecoregions derived from the WB/WWF Conservation Assessment (Dinerstein et al. 1995).

* This ecoregion designation was created for this study and does not conform to WB/WWF dataset.

# Figure 3.16  Ecoregions and Parks in Peril Sites of Venezuela

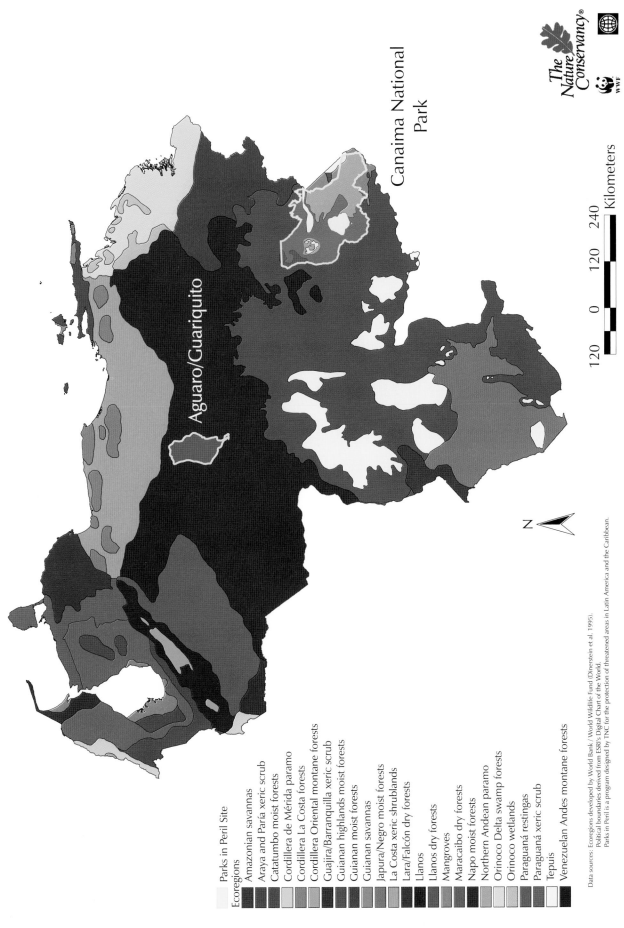

Aguaro/Guariquito

Canaima National Park

Parks in Peril Site

Ecoregions

Amazonian savannas
Araya and Pária xeric scrub
Catatumbo moist forests
Cordillera de Mérida paramo
Cordillera La Costa forests
Cordillera Oriental montane forests
Guajira/Barranquilla xeric scrub
Guianan highlands moist forests
Guianan moist forests
Guianan savannas
Japura/Negro moist forests
La Costa xeric shrublands
Lara/Falcón dry forests
Llanos
Llanos dry forests
Mangroves
Maracaibo dry forests
Napo moist forests
Northern Andean paramo
Orinoco Delta swamp forests
Orinoco wetlands
Paraguaná restingas
Paraguaná xeric scrub
Tepuis
Venezuelan Andes montane forests

120    0    120    240
Kilometers

Data sources: Ecoregions developed by World Bank / World Wildlife Fund (Dinerstein et al. 1995).
Political boundaries derived from ESRI's Digital Chart of the World.
Parks in Peril is a program designed by TNC for the protection of threatened areas in Latin America and the Caribbean.

# Figure 3.17 Migrant Species Richness in Ecoregions of Venezuela

## All Species

## Species with a South American Affinity

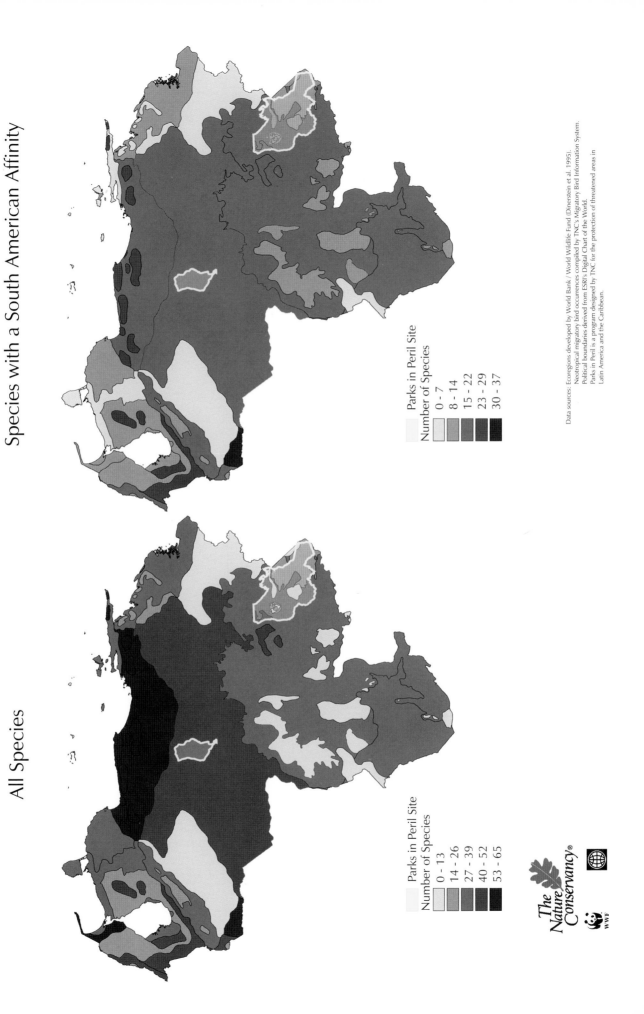

Parks in Peril Site
Number of Species
- 0 - 13
- 14 - 26
- 27 - 39
- 40 - 52
- 53 - 65

Parks in Peril Site
Number of Species
- 0 - 7
- 8 - 14
- 15 - 22
- 23 - 29
- 30 - 37

Data sources: Ecoregions developed by World Bank / World Wildlife Fund (Dinerstein et al. 1995).
Neotropical migratory bird occurrences compiled by TNC's Migratory Bird Information System.
Political boundaries derived from ESRI's Digital Chart of the World.
Parks in Peril is a program designed by TNC for the protection of threatened areas in
Latin America and the Caribbean.

# Figure 3.18   Migrant Species Richness in Ecoregions of Venezuela:
## Species of Conservation Concern

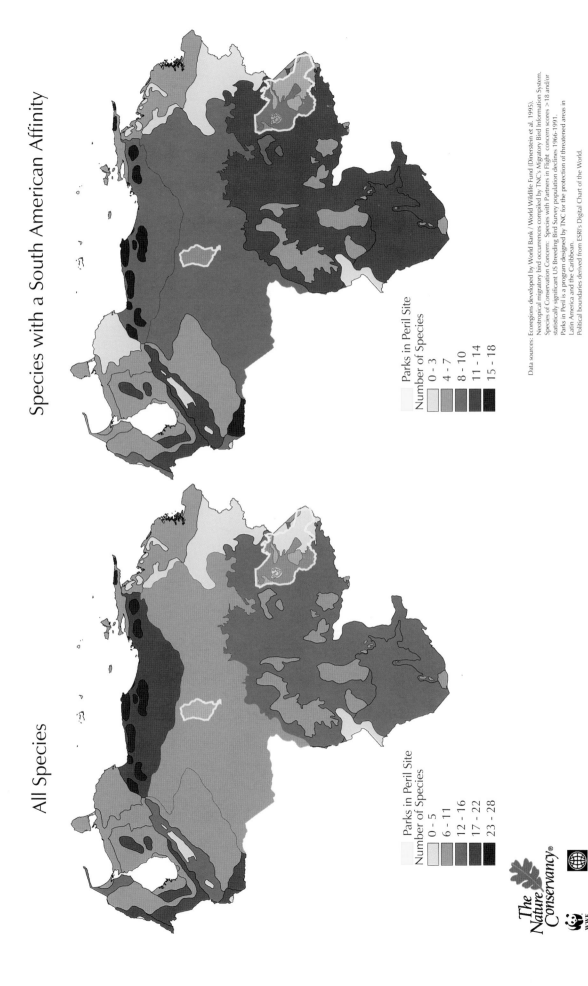

All Species

Species with a South American Affinity

Parks in Peril Site
Number of Species
0 - 5
6 - 11
12 - 16
17 - 22
23 - 28

Parks in Peril Site
Number of Species
0 - 3
4 - 7
8 - 10
11 - 14
15 - 18

Data sources: Ecoregions developed by World Bank / World Wildlife Fund (Dinerstein et al. 1995).
Neotropical migratory bird occurrences compiled by TNC's Migratory Bird Information System.
Species of Conservation Concern:  Species with Partners in Flight  concern scores >18 and/or
statistically significant US Breeding Bird Survey population declines 1966-1991.
Parks in Peril is a program designed by TNC for the protection of threatened areas in
Latin America and the Caribbean.
Political boundaries derived from ESRI's Digital Chart of the World.

The
Nature
Conservancy®

WWF

# Table 3.7  Parks in Peril Site Occurrences of Neotropical Migratory Birds

Occurrences within nations ( ◆ ) and Parks in Peril Sites (recorded = ● ; estimated = ○ ) are indicated.

| Family/Common Name | Canaima (VEN) | Aguaro (VEN) | VENEZUELA | Yanachaga (PE) | Tabaconas (PE) | Paracas[2] (PE) | Pampas (PE) | Pacaya (PE) | PERU | Mbaracayu (PY) | Defensores[2] (PY) | PARAGUAY | Yasuni (EC) | Podocarpus (EC) | Machalilla (EC) | Maquipucuna (EC) | Galap. MR (EC) | Galap. NP (EC) | Cayambe (EC) | Antisana (EC) | ECUADOR | Utria[2] (CO) | Santa Marta (CO) | La Paya (CO) | Chingaza (CO) | Cahuinari (CO) | COLOMBIA | Tariquia (BO) | Noel Kempff (BO) | Amboro (BO) | BOLIVIA | SAA[1] |
|---|---|---|---|---|---|---|---|---|---|---|---|---|---|---|---|---|---|---|---|---|---|---|---|---|---|---|---|---|---|---|---|---|
| **Storm-Petrels** | | | | | | | | | | | | | | | | | | | | | | | | | | | | | | | | |
| Leach's storm-petrel | | | ◆ | | | | | | ◆ | | | | | | | | | ● | ● | | ◆ | | | | | | ◆ | | | | | |
| black storm-petrel | | | | | | | ● | | | | | | | | | | ○ | | | | ◆ | | | | | | ◆ | | | | | |
| least storm-petrel | | | | | | | | | | | | | | | | | | | | | ◆ | | | | | | ◆ | | | | | |
| **Bitterns and Herons** | | | | | | | | | | | | | | | | | | | | | | | | | | | | | | | | |
| least bittern | | | | | | | | | | | | | | | | | | | | | | | | | | | ◆ | | | | | |
| great blue heron | ○ | ○ | ◆ | | | | | | | | | | | ○ | | | | | | | ◆ | | | ○ | | ○ | ◆ | | | | | |
| great egret | | | | | | | | | | | | | | | | | ○ | ● | ● | ○ | ◆ | ○ | | | | ○ | ◆ | | | | | |
| snowy egret | | | | | | | | | | | | | | | | | | | | | | ○ | | | | | ◆ | | | | | |
| little blue heron | ● | ● | ◆ | | | | | ● | ◆ | | | | ○ | | | | ○ | | | | ◆ | ○ | | ○ | ○ | | ◆ | | | ○ | ◆ | |
| cattle egret | ● | ● | ◆ | | | | | | | | | | ○ | | ○ | | | | | | ◆ | ○ | | ● | ○ | ○ | ◆ | | | | | |
| green heron | ● | ● | ◆ | | | | | | | | | | ○ | | | | | | | | ◆ | | | | | | ◆ | | | | | |
| **Ducks** | | | | | | | | | | | | | | | | | | | | | | | | | | | | | | | | |
| northern pintail | ○ | ● | ◆ | | | | | | | | | | | | | | | | | | | | | ○ | | ○ | ◆ | | | | | |
| blue-winged teal | ● | ● | ◆ | ● | ○ | ● | | | ◆ | | | | ○ | ○ | ○ | | ○ | ● | ● | ○ | ◆ | | | ○ | ○ | ○ | ◆ | | | | | |
| cinnamon teal | | | ◆ | | | | | | | | | | | | | | | | | | | | | | | ○ | ◆ | | | | | |
| northern shoveler | | | ◆ | | | | | | | | | | | | | | | | | | | | | ○ | | ○ | ◆ | | | | | |
| American wigeon | | | ◆ | | | | | | | | | | | | | | | | | | | | | ○ | | | ◆ | | | | | |
| lesser scaup | | | ◆ | | | | | | | | | | | | | | | | | | | | | | | | ◆ | | | | | |
| **Vultures** | | | | | | | | | | | | | | | | | | | | | | | | | | | | | | | | |
| turkey vulture | ● | ● | ◆ | ● | ● | ● | ● | ● | ◆ | ● | ● | ◆ | ● | ● | | | ○ | | | ○ | ◆ | ○ | | ● | | ○ | ◆ | ○ | ● | ● | ◆ | |

**Kites, Hawks and Ospreys**
osprey
American swallow-tailed kite
Mississippi kite
broad-winged hawk
Swainson's hawk

**Falcons**
merlin
peregrine falcon

**Rails**
sora

**Plovers**
black-bellied plover
American golden-plover
Wilson's plover
semipalmated plover
killdeer

**Sandpipers, Phalaropes and Allies**
greater yellowlegs
lesser yellowlegs
solitary sandpiper
willet
wandering tattler
spotted sandpiper
upland sandpiper
whimbrel
Hudsonian godwit
ruddy turnstone
surfbird
red knot
sanderling
semipalmated sandpiper
western sandpiper
least sandpiper

Table

3

131

Table 3.7 *Parks in Peril Site Occurrences of Neotropical Migratory Birds (continued)*

| Family/Common Name | VENEZUELA Canaima | VENEZUELA Aguaro | VEN ◆ | PERU Yanachaga | PERU Tabaconas | PERU Paracas 2 | PERU Pampas | PERU Pacaya | PERU ◆ | PARAGUAY Mbaracayu | PARAGUAY Defensores 2 | PAR ◆ | ECUADOR Yasuni | ECUADOR Podocarpus | ECUADOR Maquipucuna | ECUADOR Machalilla | ECUADOR Galap. MR | ECUADOR Galap. NP | ECUADOR Cayambe | ECUADOR Antisana | ECU ◆ | COLOMBIA Utria 2 | COLOMBIA Santa Marta | COLOMBIA La Paya | COLOMBIA Chingaza | COLOMBIA Cahuinari | COL ◆ | BOLIVIA Tariquia | BOLIVIA Noel Kempff | BOLIVIA Amboro | BOL ◆ | SAA 1 |
|---|---|---|---|---|---|---|---|---|---|---|---|---|---|---|---|---|---|---|---|---|---|---|---|---|---|---|---|---|---|---|---|---|
| white-rumped sandpiper | | ● | ◆ | | | ○ | ● | ○ | ◆ | | ○ | ◆ | ○ | ○ | ○ | | ○ | ● | ● | ● | ◆ | | | ○ | ○ | ● | ◆ | | | ○ | ◆ | ◆ |
| Baird's sandpiper | | ● | ◆ | | | ○ | ● | ○ | ◆ | | ○ | ◆ | ○ | ○ | ○ | ○ | ○ | ● | ● | ● | ◆ | | | ○ | ○ | | ◆ | | ○ | ● | ◆ | ◆ |
| pectoral sandpiper | | ○ | ◆ | | | ○ | ● | ○ | ◆ | | ○ | ◆ | ○ | ● | ● | | ○ | ○ | ○ | ● | ◆ | | | ○ | | | ◆ | ○ | ● | ○ | ◆ | ◆ |
| stilt sandpiper | | | ◆ | | | ○ | ● | ○ | ◆ | | ○ | ◆ | ○ | ○ | | | ○ | ○ | | ○ | ◆ | | | ○ | ○ | ○ | ◆ | | ○ | ○ | ◆ | ◆ |
| buff-breasted sandpiper | | | ◆ | | | | ● | ○ | ◆ | | | | | | | | | | | | ◆ | | | | | | ◆ | | | | | ◆ |
| short-billed dowitcher | | ● | ◆ | | | ○ | ● | ○ | ◆ | | ○ | ◆ | | | | | ○ | ○ | ● | | ◆ | | | ○ | ○ | ○ | ◆ | | | ○ | | ◆ |
| common snipe | | | | | ○ | | ● | ○ | | | | | | | | ○ | | | ● | ○ | | | | ○ | | | ◆ | | | ○ | | |
| Wilson's phalarope | | ● | ◆ | | | | ● | ● | ◆ | | ○ | ◆ | | | | | ○ | ● | ● | | ◆ | | | | | ○ | ◆ | | | | ◆ | ◆ |
| red-necked phalarope | | | | | | | ● | | | | | | | | | | ○ | ● | ● | | | | | | | | ◆ | | | | | |
| red phalarope | | | | | | | ● | ● | | | | | | | | | ○ | ● | ● | ○ | ◆ | | | | | | ◆ | | | | | ◆ |
| **Gulls and Terns** | | | | | | | | | | | | | | | | | | | | | | | | | | | | | | | | |
| pomarine jaeger | | | ◆ | | | | ● | | ◆ | | | | | | | | ○ | ● | ● | | ◆ | | ○ | ○ | | | ◆ | | | | | ◆ |
| parasitic jaeger | | ● | ◆ | | | | ● | | ◆ | | | | | | | ○ | ○ | ● | ● | | ◆ | | | ○ | | | ◆ | | | | | |
| long-tailed jaeger | | | | | | | ● | | ◆ | | | | | | | | ○ | | | | ◆ | | | ● | | | ◆ | | | | | ◆ |
| laughing gull | | | ◆ | | | | | | ◆ | | | | | | | | ○ | ● | ● | | ◆ | | | | | | ◆ | | | | | |
| Franklin's gull | | | | | | | ● | ○ | ◆ | | | | | | | | ○ | | | | ◆ | | ○ | ● | | | ◆ | | ◆ | | | ◆ |
| Sabine's gull | | | | | | | ● | | ◆ | | | | | | | | ○ | ● | | | | ○ | ○ | | | | ◆ | | | | | |
| gull-billed tern | | ● | ◆ | | | | ● | | ◆ | | | | | | | | ○ | | | | ◆ | | | ○ | | | ◆ | | | | | |
| royal tern | | ● | ◆ | | | | ● | | ◆ | | | | | | | | ○ | ● | ● | | ◆ | | | ● | | | ◆ | | | | | ◆ |
| elegant tern | | | | | | | ● | | ◆ | | | | | | | | ○ | | | | ◆ | | | | | | ◆ | | | | | ◆ |
| sandwich tern | | | | | | | ● | | | | | | | | | | ○ | | | | | | | | | | ◆ | | | | | |
| roseate tern | | | ◆ | | | | ● | ○ | ◆ | | | | | | | | ○ | ● | ● | | ◆ | | | ○ | | ○ | ◆ | | | | | |
| common tern | | | ◆ | | | | ● | | ◆ | | | | ○ | | | | ○ | | | | ◆ | | | | ○ | | ◆ | | | | | ◆ |
| Arctic tern | | | | | | | ● | | ◆ | | | | | | | | ○ | ● | | | ◆ | | | | | | ◆ | | | | | |
| least tern | | ● | ◆ | | | | ● | | ◆ | | | | ● | | | | ○ | ● | | | ◆ | | | ○ | | ○ | ◆ | | | | | ◆ |
| black tern | | | | | | | ● | | ◆ | | | | | | | | ○ | | | | ◆ | | | | | | ◆ | | | | | |
| **Cuckoos** | | | | | | | | | | | | | | | | | | | | | | | | | | | | | | | | |
| black-billed cuckoo | | | ◆ | ● | | ○ | ● | ○ | ◆ | ○ | ○ | ◆ | ○ | ○ | ○ | ○ | ○ | ● | ● | ○ | ◆ | | | ○ | ○ | ○ | ◆ | ○ | ○ | ● | ◆ | ◆ |
| yellow-billed cuckoo | ○ | ● | ◆ | ○ | ○ | ○ | ● | ● | ◆ | ● | ○ | ◆ | ○ | ○ | ○ | ○ | ○ | ● | ● | ○ | ◆ | ○ | | ● | ○ | ○ | ◆ | ○ | ○ | ● | ◆ | ◆ |

132   **Table   3**

**Nighthawks**
lesser nighthawk
common nighthawk
chuck-will's-widow

**Swifts**
black swift
chimney swift

**Kingfishers**
belted kingfisher

**Tyrant Flycatchers**
olive-sided flycatcher
western wood-pewee
eastern wood-pewee
acadian flycatcher
alder flycatcher
willow flycatcher
great crested flycatcher
sulphur-bellied flycatcher
eastern kingbird
gray kingbird

**Swallows**
purple martin
bank swallow
cliff swallow
barn swallow

**Thrushes**
veery
gray-cheeked thrush
Swainson's thrush

Table

3

133

**Table 3.7** *Parks in Peril Site Occurrences of Neotropical Migratory Birds (continued)*

| Family/Common Name | SAA¹ | BOLIVIA Amboro | Noel Kempff | Tariquia | COLOMBIA Cahuinari | Chingaza | La Paya | Santa Marta | Utria² | ECUADOR Antisana | Cayambe | Calap. NP | Calap. MR | Machalilla | Maquipucuna | Podocarpus | Yasuni | PARAGUAY Defensores² | Mbaracayu | PERU Pacaya | Pampas | Paracas² | Tabaconas | Yanachaga | VENEZUELA Aguaro | Canaima |
|---|---|---|---|---|---|---|---|---|---|---|---|---|---|---|---|---|---|---|---|---|---|---|---|---|---|---|
| **Vireos** | | | | | | | | | | | | | | | | | | | | | | | | | | |
| yellow-throated vireo | ◆ | | | ◆ | ◆ | ○ | ○ | ○ | ○ | ◆ | ○ | | | | ○ | ○ | ○ | | | ◆ | | ○ | ○ | ◆ | ● | |
| red-eyed vireo | ◆ | ○ | | ◆ | ◆ | ○ | ○ | ○ | ○ | ◆ | ○ | | | | ○ | ○ | | | | ◆ | | | | ◆ | ● | |
| black-whiskered vireo | ◆ | | | | ◆ | ○ | ● | ○ | | | | | | | | | | | | ◆ | | | | ◆ | | |
| yellow-green vireo | | | ○ | | ◆ | ○ | ○ | ○ | ○ | ◆ | ○ | | | | | | | | | ◆ | | | | ◆ | | |
| **Songbirds and Allies** | | | | | | | | | | | | | | | | | | | | | | | | | | |
| golden-winged warbler | | | | | ◆ | | ● | ○ | ○ | ◆ | | | | | | | | | | | | | | ◆ | ● | |
| Tennessee warbler | | | | | ◆ | ○ | ● | ○ | ○ | ◆ | ○ | ● | ○ | ● | ○ | ○ | | | | ◆ | | | | ◆ | ● | |
| yellow warbler | ◆ | | | | ◆ | ○ | ○ | ○ | ○ | ◆ | ○ | ● | ○ | ○ | ○ | ○ | ○ | | | ◆ | | ○ | ○ | ◆ | ○ ● | |
| chestnut-sided warbler | | | | | ◆ | | ○ | ○ | ○ | | | | | | | | | | | | | | | ◆ | | |
| magnolia warbler | | | | | ◆ | | | | | | | | | | | | | | | | | | | ◆ | | |
| Cape May warbler | | | | | ◆ | | | ○ | | | | | | | | | | | | | | | | ◆ | | |
| black-throated blue warbler | | | | | ◆ | | ○ | | | | | | | | | | | | | | | | | ◆ | | |
| yellow-rumped warbler | | | | | ◆ | | | ○ | | | | | | | | | | | | | | | | ◆ | | |
| black-throated green warbler | ◆ | | | | ◆ | ○ | ○ | ○ | ○ | ◆ | ○ | | | ● | ● | ● | ○ | | | ◆ | | ● | ● | ◆ | ● | |
| blackburnian warbler | ◆ | | | | ◆ | ● | ● | ○ | ○ | ◆ | ● | | | ● | ● | ● | ● | | | ◆ | ● | ○ | ● | ◆ | ● ● | |
| bay-breasted warbler | ◆ | | | | ◆ | ○ | ● | ● | ○ | ◆ | ○ | | | ○ | ● | ● | | | | ◆ | | ○ | | ◆ | ● ● | |
| blackpoll warbler | | | | | ◆ | ○ | ○ | ○ | ○ | ◆ | ● | | | ● | ● | ● | ○ | | | ◆ | | ○ | ● | ◆ | ● ● | |
| cerulean warbler | | | | | ◆ | ○ | ○ | ○ | ○ | | | | | ● | ○ | ○ | ○ | | | ◆ | | ○ | ● | ◆ | ○ ● | |
| black-and-white warbler | ◆ | | | ◆ | ◆ | ○ | ○ | ○ | ○ | ◆ | ○ | | | | ● | ○ | ○ | | | ◆ | | | | ◆ | ○ | |
| American redstart | | | | | ◆ | ○ | ● | ● | ○ | ◆ | ● | | | ○ | ● | ○ | ○ | | | ◆ | | ○ | | ◆ | ● | |
| prothonotary warbler | | | | | ◆ | | ○ | | ○ | | | | | | | | | | | | | ○ | | ◆ | | |
| ovenbird | | | | | ◆ | ○ | ○ | ○ | | | | | | | | | | | | | | | | ◆ | | |
| northern waterthrush | ◆ | | | ◆ | ◆ | ○ | ● | ○ | ○ | ◆ | ● | | | ● | ○ | ○ | ○ | | | ◆ | | ○ | | ◆ | ● | |
| Louisiana waterthrush | | | | | ◆ | ○ | ○ | ○ | | | | | | | | | | | | | | | | ◆ | ● | |
| Kentucky warbler | | | | | ◆ | | ● | ○ | | | | | | | | | | | | | | | | ◆ | ● | |
| Connecticut warbler | | | | | ◆ | ○ | ○ | | | | | | | | | | | | | | | | | ◆ | ○ | |
| mourning warbler | ◆ | | | | ◆ | ○ | ○ | ○ | ○ | ◆ | ● | | | | ○ | ○ | ○ | | | ◆ | | | | ◆ | ○ | |
| common yellowthroat | ◆ | | | | ◆ | | ○ | ○ | | ◆ | | | | | | | | | | ◆ | | | | ◆ | | |

## Songbirds and Allies (continued)

hooded warbler

Canada warbler

summer tanager

scarlet tanager

rose-breasted grosbeak

dickcissel

bobolink

orchard oriole

northern oriole

**Total:** 53  43  41  33  23  131  32  65  56  93  63  97  54  54  46  62  43  49  52  28  27  24  84  51  45  54  46  39  111  46  62

[1] Neotropical Migratory Bird with a South American Affinity.

[2] Potential Parks in Peril Site.

♦ = National occurrence.

● = Recorded park occurrence.

○ = Estimated park occurrence based upon ecoregion information.

# Chapter 4

# Habitat Preferences and Threats

The regional and national assessments presented in the two previous chapters address the question, "What birds might we lose?" The next step is to discuss two additional questions, "How might we lose them, and why?"

As mentioned earlier, the decline of many populations of neotropical migrants in the United States has been clearly demonstrated through long-term studies.[82] Some migratory species may be more vulnerable to extinction than are birds that spend their entire lives only in tropical zones or only in temperate areas. The reason is that the multiple habitats that many migrants need represent "fragile links," as one author calls them, in a chain in which each stopover is essential. If any one link is destroyed, the migrant may not be able to complete its annual flight and will not survive.[83]

## Breeding Habitats

On breeding grounds, the main culprit appears to be the fragmentation of forest habitats.[84] Urbanization, agricultural use, and other land development contribute to this destruction so that birds find it progressively more difficult to nest successfully. The national forests of the United States, for example, are fragmented by nearly 360,000 miles of roads, which is more than eight times the total mileage in the Interstate highway system.[85] Fragmented forests not only reduce the habitat available for nesting, but also create conditions that favor predators and parasites that attack birds. Both can lead to a further decrease in nesting success.[86]

A number of additional destructive practices are altering habitats and adversely affecting breeding bird populations. Examples are the suppression of natural fires, the razing of sage and mesquite scrub to maintain rangeland, and the elimination of hedgerows by farmers.[87] Even white-tailed deer grazing on the forest's understory can be responsible for decreasing the habitat needed by bird populations.[88]

Finally, draining wetlands and developing the shores of estuaries also reduce available habitat for some breeding birds. The United States has lost 117 million acres of wetlands. More than 50 percent of the marshes, swamps, and other wetland ecosystems that were present when the Europeans arrived are gone.[89]

A recent study by Defenders of Wildlife reveals that the United States faces the loss of hundreds of natural ecosystems. The organization identifies 21 that are most endangered.[90] These imperiled ecosystems represent all types, including coastal communities, grasslands, wetlands, scrub, and deciduous, dry, and pine forests.

## Nonbreeding Habitat Use

Threats to the breeding grounds of migratory birds are only part of the story. The birds are declining as a result of conditions along their migratory routes and on nonbreeding grounds as well. In fact, some scientists believe that habitat loss in the neotropics is the single most probable cause of population declines for many migrants.[91]

The challenge ahead for ornithologists and conservationists in the ASC Region is to increase basic understanding of the patterns of distribution, abundance, and conservation status of birds in regional systems and protected areas. To help meet this challenge, we examined the threats that face transients and nonbreeding winter residents of the ASC Region.

However, prior to reviewing these threats, it is important to understand the habitat preferences of neotropical migratory birds in Latin America. These preferences explain the significance of habitat degradation and loss. Understanding of habitat preferences is crucial for directing conservation efforts.

Variations in habitat that arise from differences in soil characteristics, elevation, human disturbance, and hydrographic features are among the influences that affect the distribution of birds. Factors that are strongly influential at the local level (i.e., on a finer scale than ecoregions) include aquatic features and human alterations. Conservationists need to consider these major influences when developing strategies for action.[92]

In the present analysis, we categorized the general occurrence of species in specific aquatic and disturbed habitats. (See Table 4.1.) Six general types of aquatic habitats, such as rocky coastal shores and inland freshwater marshes, and five kinds of disturbed habitats, such as pastures or agricultural fields, are evaluated in terms of use by all the bird families that occur in the ASC Region.

## Aquatic Habitats

The study found that representatives of 11 of the 19 taxonomic families of neotropical migratory birds use one or more of the aquatic habitat categories. Eight other families of neotropical migrants were not found in aquatic habitats: storm-petrels,[93] vultures, cuckoos, nighthawks, swifts, tyrant flycatchers, thrushes, and vireos. (See Table 4.1.)

Coastal shores, both rocky and sandy, are frequented most heavily by species belonging to the plover family; the family of sandpipers, phalaropes, and their allies; and the gulls and terns family. Coastal lagoons and mudflats attract many species belonging to these families as well as species of ducks, swallows, and bitterns and herons. In addition, the rail, kingfisher, and songbird families each have one representative species that frequents coastal lagoons and mudflats. The osprey and peregrine falcon also use all of these coastal aquatic habitats.

Turning to inland aquatic habitats, we found that freshwater marshes are used regularly by a total of 40 migratory species representing all of the families found in aquatic habitats. Inland lakes and ponds are visited by 45 species from all aquatic families. The inland riverine areas are used by 40 species from all of the families except for the rails.

The migratory bird species that frequent aquatic habitats are particularly vulnerable to poisoning. The reason is that contaminants are carried by runoff into aquatic systems where migrants concentrate.[94]

## Disturbed Habitats

The ability of birds to make use of habitats altered by humans varies with species. We found that some migrants are common to abundant in disturbed habitats in the ASC Region. Conservationists may do well to capitalize on this ability of some species to adapt well to these secondary habitats. As pointed out by Ridgely and Tudor, these are the birds that:

> . . . inevitably will become the most familiar to the greatest number of people, and it is worth emphasizing that given a little encouragement, quite a large range of species can adapt to man-altered environments, though they will fail to persist in areas in which any vestige of natural habitat has been essentially obliterated.[95]

The species that neither use nor tolerate disturbed habitats of any kind are particularly vulnerable to human-caused alterations. The survival of such species as the ovenbird and cerulean warbler depends on the preservation of original habitats in the ecoregions that they use during the nonbreeding season. More research is urgently needed on the use of disturbed habitats by neotropical migrants to ensure effective conservation of this group as a whole.

The research for the present study indicates that 85 of the 132 neotropical migratory birds of interest occur in disturbed habitats in the ASC Region. (See Table 4.1.) These 85 species represent 15 taxonomic families. Those that are notably absent are the storm-petrels, ducks, cuckoos, and kingfishers.

Of the five categories of disturbed habitat, secondary woodland apparently hosts the greatest number (43 species) of migratory species. Presumably the reason is that secondary woodland most closely approximates the primary forest that originally dominated the ASC Region. Next to secondary woodlands, agricultural fields host 41 migratory species, and the plantations as a group (including lands dedicated to agroforestry) have 40 species. Another 31 species occur in pastures. Urban habitats were found to support only 23 migratory species.

The overall high number (85 of 132 species) of neotropical migrants that occur in disturbed habitats would seem to support the traditional belief that these migrants "fit in" to the resident bird community mainly by utilizing disturbed, marginal, or ephemeral habitats.[96] Current research, however, supports a different view of the relationship between neotropical migrants and tropical ecosystems. In this new paradigm, the migrants are seen as significant components of the tropical community, fitting into niches unoccupied by the tropical residents.[97]

This view is consistent with the taxonomic evidence that most neotropical migrants have ancestral roots in the neotropics. It also offers a new perspective on migrants that occur in high numbers in disturbed habitats. Research on selected migrants at certain primary and disturbed sites in the neotropics indicates that some birds are overcrowded and are not finding enough resources.[98] Many species may be producing more offspring on the breeding grounds than can be supported on the nonbreeding grounds. High migrant densities in disturbed habitats on the nonbreeding grounds thus may reflect overcrowding rather than any inherent suitability of disturbed habitats. In addition, there is evidence that disturbed habitats do not fully provide for the needs of the reported 85 neotropical migratory species.[99] Given the accelerated rate of habitat loss in South America, the need is urgent for research to distinguish between those neotropical migrants that thrive in disturbed habitats versus those that have been crowded out of their preferred habitat.

© Hermes Justiniano

*Some neotropical migratory species thrive in disturbed habitats, but fragmented landscapes filter out a significant number of migrants that prefer primary, undisturbed habitats.*

The suitability of disturbed habitats is most probably related to the original or "primordial" habitat in which a species evolved.[100] For example, the primordial habitat for some field-associated migrant species, such as the dickcissel, was probably various open habitats such as the llanos, which have features in common with certain kinds of agricultural cropland. For other species that now occur in agricultural fields, plantations, and secondary woodlands, such as the rose-breasted grosbeak, the primordial habitat was probably forest. Their ability to use more marginal habitats labels these primordial species as "flexible." Yet it appears that this group of species still requires at least some exposure to original forest, given the high densities of these birds reported in forest patches.

Species richness in disturbed habitats should not give conservationists a feeling of complacency. Despite the relatively high abundance and species diversity in some early successional habitats compared with mature moist forest, most species using the successional disturbed habitats are edge or forest border species. Apart from a few exceptions such as the chestnut-sided warbler, these species need mature forest to maintain their numbers in the disturbed sites.[101]

With regard to the sometimes great abundance of migrants in agricultural fields, it is important to distinguish numbers of individuals from numbers of species. Although the number of individuals may be high in a rice field, for example, in many cases the number of species in agricultural settings is low compared with the forest from which the fields were carved.[102]

## Coffee, Cacao, and Citrus Plantations

Use of one category of disturbed habitat, the various kinds of plantations, warrants a closer look. Vast portions of Latin America are being converted to agriculture, and the survival of neotropical migrants in these rapidly changing areas is highly dependent on the migratory species and the kind of crop.

It has been discovered that plantations, particularly those growing cacao or coffee, "are often surprisingly rich in birdlife"[103] when compared with other types of crops. Across Latin America, certain neotropical migrants on plantations have been found in relatively large numbers, especially in arboreal agriculture such as pine, cacao, and shade coffee. Studies by Russell Greenberg on coffee plantations in Central America have shown that traditional coffee plantations support high diversity and overall densities of migratory birds, as well as the highest densities for certain species.[104] In fact, in a survey of neotropical migrants in various kinds of plantations, shade coffee and cacao (grown under a canopy) came closest to matching the bird populations of mature broadleaf forest.[105]

Other crops where certain migrants are common include cashew, mango, rice plantations, and citrus plots. Some nectar feeders in Central America are actually more common in citrus or cacao agriculture than they are in the forest. Species that do not seem to do well in plantation habitats are ground-feeding birds, which are found to be scarce or absent due to the lack of a dense understory.[106] Agricultural practices also affect birdlife. Full-sun coffee plantations yield five times more beans than shaded plantations but offer suboptimal habitat for most wildlife, including birds. Unfortunately, the trend is now toward conversion of plantations to full-sun, and most coffee grown in South America is now the full-sun variety.

## Migrant Sensitivity to Habitat Alteration

Understanding the sensitivity of migratory birds to alterations in their habitats is the key to recognizing their vulnerability on their nonbreeding grounds. Using a variety of literature sources, we have made a preliminary compilation of several characteristics that affect survival of migrants during the nonbreeding season in Latin America. Each of these characteristics impact the sensitivity of a given species to habitat degradation along its migratory route and at its nonbreeding destination. Unfortunately, these indicators are not available for all 132 species of migrants. Nor are they universally applicable to all species.

Despite these limitations, the indicators provide a preliminary tool for identifying species that possess particular sensitivity to habitat alteration. (See Table 2.1.) The indicators of vulnerability on nonbreeding grounds include habitat specialization, preference for primary habitat, nonbreeding site fidelity, and vulnerability to tropical deforestation.

A bird that is a habitat specialist—i.e., generally uses only one particular habitat—on its nonbreeding grounds is vulnerable to habitat degradation and destruction. If the habitat disappears, then the bird may not survive the nonbreeding season. Sixteen species of landbirds have been identified as habitat specialists on various nonbreeding grounds in Latin America. Of these, four species have been categorized as habitat generalists, however, in other studies. This seeming discrepancy illustrates the point that habitat preferences during the nonbreeding season are not fixed for all migrants. Physical condition, sex, and age affect habitat selection.[107] Moreover, some species may be specialists when

visiting some nations and show generalist tendencies in others.

The second indicator is definite preference for habitats with primary vegetation, as opposed to secondary or altered habitat. A species that prefers primary habitat is also vulnerable during its sojourn in Latin America. Primary vegetation of most types is disappearing rapidly. Table 2.1 shows 30 species of landbirds and waterfowl that are found only rarely in areas other than primary vegetation habitats.

Site fidelity, the tendency for an individual bird to maintain a distinct home range throughout a season and return to it in successive years, is another characteristic that is believed to put birds at greater risk for survival if the habitat is altered. Fidelity to the nonbreeding site has been documented for 45 of the migratory bird species that occur regularly in the ASC Region. Of these, 15 are migrants with a South American affinity. (See Table 2.1.)

This finding that more than one-third of all migrants to the ASC Region exhibit site fidelity to some degree has powerful implications for conservation of these birds. This is especially true, considering that this type of information is not yet available for many species. One study performed in isolated and extensive forests documented a high return rate (up to 50 percent) for some banded neotropical migrants in successive years.[108] Unfortunately, this kind of information requires long-term banding studies at a given site and is only available for a limited number of migratory species.

Birds that hold long-term home ranges to which they return year after year certainly do not fit the traditional view of migrants as "marginal" and "flexible" species that are tolerant to alterations in habitat. It is highly

*Slash-and-burn is commonly used in many countries as an agricultural technique. Burning off forests to create fields is responsible for much of the accelerated deforestation that is occurring in Latin America and the Caribbean, and it is one of the major causes of the decline of neotropical migratory birds.*

likely that the list of birds exhibiting nonbreeding site fidelity will enlarge substantially as more studies are conducted.

Eugene Morton identified 13 species of migratory landbirds as vulnerable to deforestation, the fourth indicator.[109] (See Table 2.1.) Morton based this designation on wintering site specificity, social tolerance, diet and foraging specialization, and the ability to use non-forest habitat.

An overview of the habitat sensitivity indicators (see Table 2.1) reveals that 58 neotropical migrants have one or more of the four positive indicators. Of these, 19 are neotropical migrants with a South American

affinity, which means that more than one-third of this special group of 53 species are particularly sensitive to habitat alteration during the nonbreeding season. Our evaluation is surely conservative, because the supporting data for many species is lacking.

## Habitat Threats

The ability of neotropical migratory birds to survive the challenges of long-distance migration between separate and ecologically different breeding and nonbreeding grounds results from an evolutionary process that involved many generations of birds going back thousands of years. The loss of species with this amazing ability may take only decades of habitat degradation and destruction.

The major factors in Latin America contributing to population declines of neotropical migratory birds are deforestation, draining of wetlands, and other forms of habitat destruction.[110] Additional factors, such as pesticide use, exacerbate the adverse effects of habitat loss.

Because of the lack of available information, the conservation community appears to have a poor knowledge of the extent and diversity of threats to migratory birds during the nonbreeding season in Latin America. But the impetus for action is clear: The populations of many resident and migratory species have declined, and many more may become endangered unless adequate conservation measures are taken. Filling the gaps in information on habitat threats is a vital step if programs to protect avian habitats are to be successful.

The team that developed the World Bank-World Wildlife Fund ecoregion classification scheme took some significant steps toward identifying habitat threats in Latin America. When the team members developed the ecoregion scheme, they assigned a "final conservation status" index value to the ecoregions based on a variety of factors.[111] Using these index values, the team went on to assign the ecoregions to five categories ranging from critical to relatively intact.

When we examined the team's categorization for the ecoregions occurring in the ASC Region, we found that the conservation status of 53 of these ecoregions is poor because they are in the critical, endangered, or vulnerable categories. Only 15 ecoregions in the ASC Region are considered relatively stable or intact:

| Category | Number of Ecoregions[112] |
|---|---|
| Critical | 11 |
| Endangered | 18 |
| Vulnerable | 24 |
| Relatively Stable | 11 |
| Relatively Intact | 4 |

The ecoregions that are considered critical and have the greatest numbers of neotropical migratory bird species include the Ecuadorian dry forests, Sinú Valley dry forests, Catatumbo moist forests, and western Ecuador moist forests. The ecoregions categorized as endangered and richest in species include Guajira/Barranquilla xeric scrub, La Costa xeric shrublands, northwestern Andean montane forests, and Magdalena/Urabá moist forests.

Further efforts to protect neotropical migrants in the ASC Region will need to begin with improvement in the conservation status of the ecoregions that the birds inhabit. Although some species are flexible in their use of habitats, such flexibility is neither limitless nor universal. Moreover, the rate of habitat loss and destruction far exceeds any evolutionary adaptations. Thus the fate of neotropical migrants is integrally tied to the fate of their habitats.

# Table 4.1 Occurrence of Neotropical Migrants in Aquatic and Secondary Habitats within Ecoregions

| Family/Common Name | Aquatic Habitats Coastal | | | Aquatic Habitats Inland | | | Terrestrial Habitats Secondary/Disturbed | | | | |
|---|---|---|---|---|---|---|---|---|---|---|---|
| | Rocky Shore | Sandy Shore | Lagoon/Mudflats | Freshwater Marshes | Lakes/Ponds | Riverine | Pastures | Agricultural Fields | Urban | Plantation (Agroforestry) | Secondary Woodland |
| **Storm-Petrels** | | | | | | | | | | | |
| Leach's storm-petrel | | | | | | | | | | | |
| black storm-petrel | | | | | | | | | | | |
| least storm-petrel | | | | | | | | | | | |
| **Bitterns and Herons** | | | | | | | | | | | |
| least bittern | | | | ● | ● | | ● | | | | |
| great blue heron | | ● | ● | ● | ● | ● | | | | | |
| great egret | | | ● | ● | ● | | | ● | | | |
| snowy egret | | | ● | ● | ● | | | ● | | | |
| little blue heron | ● | ● | ● | ● | ● | ● | ● | ● | | | |
| cattle egret | | | ● | ● | ● | ● | ● | ● | ● | | |
| green heron | | | ● | ● | ● | ● | | | | | |
| **Ducks** | | | | | | | | | | | |
| northern pintail | | | ● | ● | ● | | | | | | |
| blue-winged teal | | | ● | ● | ● | ● | | | | | |
| cinnamon teal | | | | ● | ● | | | | | | |
| northern shoveler | | | ● | ● | ● | | | | | | |
| American wigeon | | | ● | ● | ● | | | | | | |
| lesser scaup | | | ● | | ● | | | | | | |
| **Vultures** | | | | | | | | | | | |
| turkey vulture | | | | | | | ● | ● | ● | ● | ● |

| Family/Common Name | Aquatic Habitats Coastal | | | Inland | | | Terrestrial Habitats Secondary/Disturbed | | | | |
| --- | --- | --- | --- | --- | --- | --- | --- | --- | --- | --- | --- |
| | Rocky Shore | Sandy Shore | Lagoon/Mudflats | Freshwater Marshes | Lakes/Ponds | Riverine | Pastures | Agricultural Fields | Urban | Plantation (Agroforestry) | Secondary Woodland |
| **Kites, Hawks and Ospreys** | | | | | | | | | | | |
| osprey | • | • | • | • | • | • | | | | | |
| American swallow-tailed kite | | | | | | | | | | | |
| Mississippi kite | | | | | | | | | | | |
| broad-winged hawk | | | | | | | | • | | • | • |
| Swainson's hawk | | | | • | • | | | | | • | • |
| **Falcons** | | | | | | | | | | | |
| merlin | | | • | • | • | • | • | • | | | |
| peregrine falcon | • | • | • | • | • | • | • | • | • | | |
| **Rails** | | | | | | | | | | | |
| sora | | | • | • | • | | • | • | | | |
| **Plovers** | | | | | | | | | | | |
| black-bellied plover | • | • | • | | • | | | | | | |
| American golden-plover | | • | • | | | | | • | | | |
| Wilson's plover | • | • | • | | | | | • | | | |
| semipalmated plover | • | | | • | • | | | • | | | |
| killdeer | | | | • | • | | | | | • | • |
| **Sandpipers, Phalaropes and Allies** | | | | | | | | | | | |
| greater yellowlegs | • | • | • | • | • | • | | • | | | |
| lesser yellowlegs | | • | • | • | • | • | • | • | | | |
| solitary sandpiper | | | • | • | • | • | • | • | | | • |
| willet | • | • | • | | | | | | | | |

| Family/Common Name | Rocky Shore | Sandy Shore | Lagoon/Mudflats | Freshwater Marshes | Lakes/Ponds | Riverine | Pastures | Agricultural Fields | Urban | Plantation (Agroforestry) | Secondary Woodland |
|---|---|---|---|---|---|---|---|---|---|---|---|
| **Aquatic Habitats** | Coastal | | | Inland | | | **Terrestrial Habitats** Secondary/Disturbed | | | | |
| **Sandpipers, Phalaropes and Allies (Continued)** | | | | | | | | | | | |
| wandering tattler | ● | | | | | | | | | | |
| spotted sandpiper | ● | ● | ● | ● | ● | ● | ● | ● | | | |
| upland sandpiper | | | | | ● | | ● | ● | | | |
| whimbrel | ● | ● | ● | | ● | | | ● | | | |
| Hudsonian godwit | | | ● | | ● | ● | ● | ● | | | |
| ruddy turnstone | ● | ● | ● | | | ● | | | | | |
| surfbird | ● | | ● | | | | | | | | |
| red knot | | ● | ● | | | | | | | | |
| sanderling | ● | ● | ● | | ● | ● | | | | | |
| semipalmated sandpiper | | ● | ● | | ● | | | | | | |
| western sandpiper | | ● | ● | | | | | | | | |
| least sandpiper | | ● | ● | ● | ● | | ● | ● | | | |
| white-rumped sandpiper | | ● | ● | | ● | | ● | ● | | | |
| Baird's sandpiper | | | ● | ● | ● | ● | ● | ● | | | |
| pectoral sandpiper | | ● | ● | ● | ● | ● | ● | ● | | | |
| stilt sandpiper | | ● | ● | ● | ● | | ● | ● | | | |
| buff-breasted sandpiper | | | ● | | ● | | | ● | | | |
| short-billed dowitcher | | ● | ● | ● | | | | ● | | | |
| common snipe | | | ● | ● | ● | | ● | ● | | | |
| Wilson's phalarope | | | ● | ● | ● | | ● | ● | | | |
| red-necked phalarope | | | ● | | | | | | | | |
| red phalarope | | | ● | | | | | | | | |

*Table 4.1* Occurrence of Neotropical Migrants in Aquatic and Secondary Habitats within Ecoregions (continued)

| Family/Common Name | Aquatic Habitats | | | | | | Terrestrial Habitats | | | | |
| | Coastal | | | Inland | | | Secondary/Disturbed | | | | |
| | Rocky Shore | Sandy Shore | Lagoon/Mudflats | Freshwater Marshes | Lakes/Ponds | Riverine | Pastures | Agricultural Fields | Urban | Plantation (Agroforestry) | Secondary Woodland |
|---|---|---|---|---|---|---|---|---|---|---|---|
| **Gulls and Terns** | | | | | | | | | | | |
| pomarine jaeger | | | | | | | | | | | |
| parasitic jaeger | | | | | | | | | | | |
| long-tailed jaeger | | | | | | | | | | | |
| laughing gull | ● | ● | ● | | ● | ● | | ● | | | |
| Franklin's gull | | ● | ● | | ● | | | ● | | | |
| Sabine's gull | | | | | | | | | | | |
| gull-billed tern | | ● | ● | ● | | ● | | | | | |
| royal tern | ● | ● | ● | | | | | | | | |
| elegant tern | ● | ● | ● | | | | | | | | |
| sandwich tern | ● | ● | ● | | | | | | | | |
| roseate tern | | ● | ● | | | | | | | | |
| common tern | ● | ● | ● | | | ● | | | | | |
| arctic tern | ● | ● | | | | | | | | | |
| least tern | | ● | ● | | | | | | | | |
| black tern | ● | ● | ● | ● | ● | | | | | | |
| **Cuckoos** | | | | | | | | | | | |
| black-billed cuckoo | | | | | | | | | | | |
| yellow-billed cuckoo | | | | | | | | | | | |
| **Nighthawks** | | | | | | | | | | | |
| lesser nighthawk | | | | | | | ● | ● | | | |
| common nighthawk | | | | | | | | | ● | | |
| chuck-will's-widow | | | | | | | | ● | | ● | ● |

**Table 4.1** *Occurrence of Neotropical Migrants in Aquatic and Secondary Habitats within Ecoregions (continued)*

| Family/Common Name | Aquatic Habitats Coastal | | | Aquatic Habitats Inland | | | Terrestrial Habitats Secondary/Disturbed | | | | |
|---|---|---|---|---|---|---|---|---|---|---|---|
| | Rocky Shore | Sandy Shore | Lagoon/Mudflats | Freshwater Marshes | Lakes/Ponds | Riverine | Pastures | Agricultural Fields | Urban | Plantation (Agroforestry) | Secondary Woodland |
| **Swifts** | | | | | | | | | | | |
| black swift | | | | | | | | | | | |
| chimney swift | | | | | | | | | • | | |
| **Kingfishers** | | | | | | | | | | | |
| belted kingfisher | | | • | • | • | • | | | | | |
| **Tyrant Flycatchers** | | | | | | | | | | | |
| olive-sided flycatcher | | | | | | | | | | • | • |
| western wood-pewee | | | | | | | | | | • | • |
| eastern wood-pewee | | | | | | | | | | • | • |
| acadian flycatcher | | | | | | | | | | • | • |
| alder flycatcher | | | | | | | • | | | • | |
| willow flycatcher | | | | | | | • | | | • | |
| great crested flycatcher | | | | | | | | | | | • |
| sulphur-bellied flycatcher | | | | | | | | | | | • |
| eastern kingbird | | | | | | | • | | • | • | • |
| gray kingbird | | | | | | | • | • | • | | |
| **Swallows** | | | | | | | | | | | |
| purple martin | | • | | • | • | • | • | • | • | | |
| bank swallow | | • | | • | • | • | • | • | | | |
| cliff swallow | | • | | • | • | • | • | • | | | |
| barn swallow | | • | | • | • | • | • | • | • | | |

| | Aquatic Habitats | | | | | | Terrestrial Habitats | | | | |
| | Coastal | | | Inland | | | Secondary/Disturbed | | | | |
| Family/Common Name | Rocky Shore | Sandy Shore | Lagoon/Mudflats | Freshwater Marshes | Lakes/Ponds | Riverine | Pastures | Agricultural Fields | Urban | Plantation (Agroforestry) | Secondary Woodland |
|---|---|---|---|---|---|---|---|---|---|---|---|
| **Thrushes** | | | | | | | | | | | |
| veery | | | | | | | | | | ● | ● |
| gray-cheeked thrush | | | | | | | | | ● | ● | ● |
| Swainson's thrush | | | | | | | | | ● | ● | ● |
| | | | | | | | | | | | |
| **Vireos** | | | | | | | | | | | |
| yellow-throated vireo | | | | | | | | | | ● | ● |
| red-eyed vireo | | | | | | | | | ● | ● | ● |
| black-whiskered vireo | | | | | | | | | | ● | ● |
| yellow-green vireo | | | | | | | | | | ● | ● |
| | | | | | | | | | | | |
| **Songbirds and Allies** | | | | | | | | | | | |
| golden-winged warbler | | | | | | | | | | ● | ● |
| Tennessee warbler | | | | | | | | | ● | ● | ● |
| yellow warbler | | | | | | | | | ● | ● | ● |
| chestnut-sided warbler | | | | | | | | | | ● | ● |
| magnolia warbler | | | | | | | | | | | |
| Cape May warbler | | | | | | | | | ● | ● | ● |
| black-throated blue warbler | | | | | | | | | | | ● |
| yellow-rumped warbler | | | | | | | | | ● | ● | ● |
| black-throated green warbler | | | | | | | | | | ● | ● |
| blackburnian warbler | | | | | | | | | | ● | ● |
| bay-breasted warbler | | | | | | | | | | ● | ● |
| blackpoll warbler | | | | | | | ● | | ● | ● | ● |
| cerulean warbler | | | | | | | | | | | ● |
| black-and-white warbler | | | | | | | | | | ● | ● |
| American redstart | | | | | | | | | ● | ● | ● |

**Table 4.1** *Occurrence of Neotropical Migrants in Aquatic and Secondary Habitats within Ecoregions (continued)*

| Family/Common Name | Aquatic Habitats | | | | | | Terrestrial Habitats | | | | |
| | Coastal | | | Inland | | | Secondary/Disturbed | | | | |
| | Rocky Shore | Sandy Shore | Lagoon/Mudflats | Freshwater Marshes | Lakes/Ponds | Riverine | Pastures | Agricultural Fields | Urban | Plantation (Agroforestry) | Secondary Woodland |
|---|---|---|---|---|---|---|---|---|---|---|---|
| **Songbirds and Allies (continued)** | | | | | | | | | | | |
| prothonotary warbler | | | | | • | • | | | | • | |
| ovenbird | | | | | | | | | | | • |
| northern waterthrush | | • | | • | • | • | | | | | |
| Louisiana waterthrush | | | | | | • | | | | | • |
| Kentucky warbler | | | | | | | | | | | |
| Connecticut warbler | | | | | | | | | | | |
| mourning warbler | | | | | | • | | | | • | • |
| common yellowthroat | | | | | | | • | • | | • | • |
| hooded warbler | | | | | | | | | | | • |
| Canada warbler | | | | | | | | | | • | • |
| summer tanager | | | | • | | | | • | | • | • |
| scarlet tanager | | | | | | | | | • | • | • |
| rose-breasted grosbeak | | | | | | • | | • | | • | • |
| dickcissel | | | | | | | | • | | | |
| bobolink | | | | • | | • | • | • | | • | • |
| orchard oriole | | | | | | | | | • | • | • |
| northern oriole | | | | | | | | | • | • | • |
| Total | 21 | 34 | 59 | 40 | 45 | 40 | 31 | 41 | 23 | 40 | 44 |

Habitat information provided by R. Ridgely, J.V. Remsen, and D. Ewert, 1995.

# Chapter 5

© Roger Tory Peterson

# The Conservation Challenge

The long and perilous annual journey of the neotropical migratory birds underscores the need for new conservation alliances in the Americas. The migrants symbolize the reasons why North Americans cannot turn their backs on the pressing problems of habitat degradation in Latin America. "Our birds" depend on "their land" for continued survival.

The land in this case is not a single preserve but rather an entire chain of linked stopover points and nonbreeding destinations spanning thousands of miles into South America. Migratory species face threats that extend beyond individual national boundaries. The survival of these species can be ensured only by a network of partners working together. Protecting critical nonbreeding areas, stopover sites, and breeding areas should be the paramount goal of this network.

## The Ecoregional Approach

Bird lovers in North America want to know, "Where do 'our birds' go during the winter?" In answering this question, we used a new ecoregional approach to understand bird distributions in the Andean/Southern Cone (ASC) Region of South America. This new approach involves layers of data compiled into what we believe is an accurate picture of the neotropical migratory birds of the ASC Region. In the near future, this procedure is expected to stimulate expanded conservation activities, such as prioritization for conservation and subsequent linking of sites.

Never before have universities, scientists, and The Nature Conservancy's partner organizations come together in such a mass cooperative effort to learn exactly where the neotropical migrants seek refuge in the ASC Region. Latin American partners contributed enormously to achieving the study's objectives through their knowledge, enthusiasm, and vision.

## The Plight of Neotropical Migrants

The study highlights the fact that the ASC Region is the main destination for 53 species with a South American affinity. Two-thirds of these species have a tenuous future unless their status can be improved. More than one-third (19 species) have life histories that make them especially vulnerable to habitat degradation in South America. Unfortunately, of the 68 terrestrial ecoregions in the ASC Region, only 15 are considered "relatively stable" or better.

The futures of the Franklin's gull, Mississippi kite, yellow-billed cuckoo, cerulean warbler, scarlet tanager, Canada warbler, olive-sided flycatcher, eastern wood-pewee, veery, and dickcissel—to mention a few examples—are uncertain. Protection programs for migratory birds are unlikely to be successful if we wait until only a few, isolated populations of a species remain.

The fate of the passenger pigeon, Carolina parakeet, dusky seaside sparrow, and California condor should remind us that conservation programs for birds are complex, both temporally and spatially. Protection must begin before populations are precipitously low.

Birds pose difficult conservation issues that require new thinking and new approaches. We must address migratory birds on spatial scales unlike those needed for nonmigratory animals and most plant communities. Waiting for a bird species to reach a globally distinctive endangered status historically has been a recipe for great expense and high probability of failure.

The Nature Conservancy and its partners in the Migratory Bird Initiative should step up to the challenge of preventing this scenario while the species in question remain relatively common. The challenge is to look far enough ahead to ensure success.

## Where Do We Go from Here?

The ecoregional approach has resulted in preliminary bird occurrence lists for each Parks in Peril site. We look forward to confirming occurrences in these parks based on future input from The Nature Conservancy's partners. Perhaps other protected areas will benefit as well from this concerted effort. On-the-ground refinement of bird occurrences in ecoregions and Parks in Peril sites is needed in particular for the Tariquia site in Bolivia, Defensores del Chaco in Paraguay, and all Parks in Peril sites in Colombia, excluding Sierra Nevada de Santa Marta.

Continued integration of information on endemic and resident birds is another need, as well as integration of data on other animals and communities. Analysis and prioritization of flyway use, concentration areas, and stopover sites will help in the development of linkages between sites on breeding and nonbreeding grounds. This information is crucial to identifying key areas for conservation.

In addition, projects need to be initiated to determine bird abundances in sites and ecoregions. These data are necessary to lay the groundwork for further prioritization plans for ecoregions and individual sites.

The Nature Conservancy supports an integrated approach to site selection.

At the same time, expansion and consolidation of partnerships in South America will help to facilitate the sharing of vital information on migratory birds. Communication is essential also on funding opportunities, projects, surveys, and the results of monitoring and management activities. Training workshops in theory, practice, survey methodology, and field work are needed as well. Another highly important endeavor will be support of partnerships to promote education on land-use practices beneficial to migratory birds. For example, farmers and coffee consumers alike need to be educated on the benefits of shade-grown coffee.

© Juanita Thigpen

*The survival of neotropical migratory birds depends on new alliances such as those generated by the Migratory Bird Initiative. If our winged friends are to return from afar every year, it will be because each of us helps them make the trip.*

Additional activities are necessary in the ASC Region and beyond, and The Nature Conservancy would like to undertake these projects in the longer term. The studies that are needed encompass expansion of this ecoregional methodology to the entire western hemisphere, including breeding grounds in North America and additional nonbreeding regions of Latin America.

Crucial to future conservation planning for migratory birds will be analysis of the results from desperately needed field research directed at characterizing the relative suitability of various human-altered landscapes in Latin America for each migrant species. Only with this information can we evaluate "how much is enough" in terms of conservation of the habitat types that are currently limiting the populations of these species.

## A Global Outlook

For many species of neotropical migratory birds, long-term survival depends on the quality of their habitats in several countries. Any successful preservation plan for these species will require habitat-based conservation actions that cross national boundaries.

In the past, efforts to develop conservation priorities for nonbreeding habitats of neotropical migrants have been fragmented and unsystematic. Preservation efforts have lacked a globally oriented approach that takes into account conservation needs of a range of species across an entire region. The present study is a first step toward developing this international perspective.

For neotropical migrants, the great challenge is to develop and implement solid conservation plans based on good science and partnerships among all nations that provide homes for migratory birds. The Nature Conservancy is meeting this challenge through its new Migratory Bird Initiative. The present study has focused on two objectives: determining the distribution and conservation status of neotropical migrants through an ecoregion approach and encouraging hemispheric partnerships through participation in the Migratory Bird Initiative.

A globally oriented viewpoint is imperative if these migratory fliers are to continue to make their incredible journeys. A global viewpoint and a systematic methodology based on ecoregions can do the job, however, only if they lead to conservation action.

We can save our beloved migratory birds only by working together, all the nations of the Americas. If our winged friends are to return from afar every year, it will be because each of us helps them make the trip.

# GLOSSARY

**Andean/Southern Cone (ASC) Region**
A region of The Nature Conservancy's Latin America and Caribbean Division, comprising the countries of Bolivia, Colombia, Ecuador, Paraguay, Peru, and Venezuela.

**Austral Migratory Bird**
Any species for which all or any part of its breeding range lies south of the Tropic of Capricorn and which migrates or withdraws northward during the austral winter.[113]

**Biological and Conservation Data System (BCD)**
The Nature Conservancy's PC-based data management package facilitates the collection, distribution, and exchange of information pertinent to the preservation of biological diversity.

**Breeding Bird Survey (BBS)**
The North American Breeding Bird Survey, coordinated by the U.S. Fish and Wildlife Service and the Canadian Wildlife Service, provides long-term information about the abundance and distribution of breeding birds in the United States and Canada.

**Cerrado**
A mosaic of savanna and dry forests, one of the largest savanna-forest complexes in the world.[114]

**Chaco**
A large expanse of arid scrubland and low woodland[115] extending from Bolivia through Paraguay to Argentina.[116]

**Conservation Concern**
An all-encompassing term to designate species that have a high Partners in Flight concern score and/or significantly declining BBS population trends.

**Disturbed Habitat**
Habitat that has resulted from disruption to the pattern of an ecosystem by some physical force such as fire, wind, or timber harvesting.

**Dry Forests**
Closed canopy tropical forests that are dominated by deciduous broadleaf species.[117]

## Ecoregion
A geographically distinct assemblage of natural communities that historically share a large majority of their species, exhibit similar ecological dynamics and environmental conditions, and depend for their long-term persistence on critical ecological interactions.

## Endemic
A species that is endemic to a region is a native species that occurs naturally in only one geographic area in the world.

## Flooded Grasslands
Grassy areas that are often inundated with water.[118]

## Gallery Forests
Narrow strips of forest along the margins of rivers in otherwise unwooded landscapes.[119]

## Geographic Information System
Computer software that is used to manipulate and manage geographical databases.

## Habitat Specialist
A species that generally uses only one kind of habitat.

## Llanos
A mosaic of gallery forests, dry forests, grasslands, and wetlands—the largest savanna ecosystem of northern South America.[120]

## Mangroves
Salt-tolerant forest ecosystems that occupy coastal estuarine, lagoon, deltaic, or carbonate environments.[121]

## Migratory Bird Information System
A Microsoft Access® Database that is used to integrate various information on migratory birds.

## Moist Forests
Closed canopy tropical forests that are dominated by broadleaf species.[122]

## Montane Forests
High-elevation broadleaf tropical moist forests.[123]

## Neotropical Migratory Bird
A bird that breeds, at least to some extent, in North America and spends the nonbreeding season in Mexico, Central America, the Caribbean, and/or South America.

**Neotropics**
The portion of the western hemisphere lying between the Tropic of Cancer and the Tropic of Capricorn.

**Nonbreeding Site Fidelity**
The tendency for a bird to return to the same exact nonbreeding site year after year.

**Pantanal**
A mosaic of flooded grasslands, savannas, gallery forests, and dry forests—one of the world's largest wetland complexes.[124]

**Paramo**
Wet, tropical grassland-savanna habitats found above the treeline in the Andes.[125]

**Parks in Peril Program (PiP)**
An emergency effort by The Nature Conservancy and its Latin American and Caribbean partners to safeguard the most important and imperiled natural areas in the hemisphere. The program currently includes a total of 61 sites, and USAID is the primary support of a subset of 28 of these sites.

**Partners in Flight (PIF)**
A consortium developed by the National Fish and Wildlife Foundation to bring together the collective resources of all groups interested in migratory birds and their habitats, and to promote the conservation of species while they are still common, focusing on habitats rather than single species.

**Primary Habitat**
The original old-growth habitat that exists before disturbance occurs and leads into the succession process and secondary habitat.

**Puna**
Montane grasslands of the central and southern High Andes.[126]

**Restingas**
Coastal dune or sandy soil habitats.[127]

**Savanna**
Tropical grassland ecosystems with scattered trees and shrubs.[128]

**Secondary Habitat**
A stage in succession resulting from a disturbance to the habitat; succession that has started on a disturbed site that had already supported vegetation.

**South American Affinity**
A term used to define a migratory bird for which South America is its main wintering ground, as opposed to the main wintering ground being somewhere in Mexico, Central America, or the Caribbean.

**Species Richness**
Number of species, as opposed to number of individuals.

**Succession**
The replacement of one community by another over time.

**Swamp Forests**
Lowland forests that are usually flooded due to poor drainage.[129]

**Tepuis**
Sandstone plateaus that reach several thousand meters above surrounding lowlands.[130]

**United States Agency for International Development (USAID)**
USAID is the principal source of U.S. assistance to developing countries and countries with economies in transition. The agency provides opportunities for sustainable development, including conserving biological diversity.

**Varzea**
Amazon Basin forests that are seasonally flooded.[131]

**Vulnerability on Nonbreeding Grounds**
An all-encompassing term for a species that is sensitive to habitat degradation as measured by at least one of the following: habitat specialization, preference for primary habitat, nonbreeding site fidelity, or vulnerability to tropical deforestation.

**Vulnerability to Tropical Deforestation**
Describes a species that is particularly susceptible to deforestation because it cannot survive in any habitat other than forests, unlike species that will accept disturbed habitat under the same circumstances.

**World Bank/World Wildlife Fund Conservation Priority Assessment**
A priority-setting study that elevates, as a first principle, maintenance of representation of all ecosystems and habitat types in regional investment portfolios and recognizes landscape-level features as an essential guide for effective conservation planning.

**Xeric Scrub**
Dryland and desert areas dominated by scrub and shrub species.[132]

# APPENDIX

## Austral Migrants for Continental South America: A Preliminary List

The term austral migrant, as defined here, includes any species in which all, or any part, of its breeding range lies south of the Tropic of Capricorn, and which migrates or withdraws northward during the austral winter. An austral species does not necessarily have to migrate northward into tropical latitudes, although many do (especially the Passeriformes species).

The following list does not include altitudinal migrants, such as the Andean goose and white-bellied seedsnipe, which breed at high elevations in the Andes and move to lower elevations during the coldest months.

The non-Passeriformes list does not include any species that breed only in the northern hemisphere and spend all or part of their nonbreeding season in austral latitudes. Several groups were omitted because sufficient information is currently unavailable.

The list was compiled by Steven Hilty except for the species indicated by a bullet (•). Those species are additions drawn from a list by Chesser (1994).

The asterisk (*) symbol indicates that a question exists about the bird's status as an austral migrant. The species may be only nomadic, show marked post-breeding dispersal, or simply be suspected as a migrant.

## Non-Passeriformes

| | | | |
|---|---|---|---|
| Podiceps occipitalis | Silvery grebe | Dendrocygna autumnalis | Black-bellied whistling-duck |
| Podiceps rolland | White-tufted grebe | Dendrocygna bicolor | Fulvous whistling-duck |
| Podiceps gallardoi | Hooded grebe | Dendrocygna viduata | White-faced whistling-duck |
| Podiceps major | Great grebe | Coscoroba coscoroba | Coscoroba swan |
| Podilymbus podiceps | Pied-billed grebe | Cygnus melanocorypha | Black-necked swan |
| • Phalacrocorax atriceps | Imperial shag | Chloephaga poliocephala | Ashy-headed goose |
| • Phalacrocorax magellanicus | Rock shag | Chloephaga rubidiceps | Ruddy-headed goose |
| Egretta alba | Great egret | Chloephaga picta | Upland goose |
| Egretta thula | Snowy egret | Tachyeres patachonicus | Flying steamer-duck |
| Ardea cocoi | White-necked heron | • Callonetta leucophrys | Ringed teal |
| Bubulcus ibis | Cattle egret | Anas specularioides | Crested duck |
| • Ardeola striata | Striated heron | Anas specularis | Spectacled duck |
| Tigrisoma lineatum | Rufescent tiger-heron | Anas sibilatrix | Chiloe wigeon |
| Syrigma sibilatrix | Whistling heron | Anas bahamensis | White-cheeked pintail |
| Nycticorax nycticorax | Black-crowned night heron | Anas georgica | Yellow-billed pintail |
| Ixobrychus involucris | Stripe-backed bittern | Anas flavirostris | Speckled teal |
| Jabiru mycteria | *Jabiru | Anas versicolor | Silver teal |
| Euxenura americana | Maguari stork | Anas cyanoptera | Cinnamon teal |
| Theristicus melanopis | Black-faced ibis | Anas platalea | Red shoveler |
| Phimosus infuscatus | Bare-faced (whispering) ibis | Anas leucophrys | Ringed Teal |
| Plegadis chihi | White-faced ibis | Netta peposaca | Rosy-billed pochard |
| Ajaja ajaja | Roseate spoonbill | Amazonetta brasiliensis | *Brazilian duck |
| Phoenicopterus chilensis | Chilean flamingo | Oxyura andina | *Andean duck |
| • Mycteria americana | Wood stork | Oxyura vittata | Lake duck |
| Sarkidiornis melanotos | Comb duck | Oxyura dominica | *Masked duck |

| | |
|---|---|
| Heteronetta atricapilla | Black-headed duck |
| Cathartes aura | Turkey vulture |
| Coragyps atratus | Black vulture |
| Elanoides forficatus | Swallow-tailed kite |
| Elanus leucurus | White-tailed kite |
| Ictinia plumbea | Plumbeous kite |
| Rostrhamus sociabilis | Snail kite |
| • Buteo albicaudatus | White-tailed hawk |
| Buteo polysoma | Red-backed hawk |
| Circus cinereus | Cinereous harrier |
| Circus buffoni | Long-winged harrier |
| • Accipiter striatus | Sharp-shinned hawk |
| • Accipiter bicolor | Bicolored hawk |
| • Milvago chimango | Chimango caracara |
| • Falco femoralis | Aplomado falcon |
| Falco peregrinus | Peregrine falcon |
| • Rallus sanguinolentus | Plumbeous rail |
| • Coturnicops notata | Speckled rail |
| • Gallinula chloropus | Common moorhen |
| • Porphyrula martinica | Purple gallinule |
| • Porphyrula flavirostris | Azure gallinule |
| • Fulica armillata | Red-gartered coot |
| • Fulica leucoptera | White-winged coot |
| Aramus guarauna | *Limpkin |
| Nycticryphes semicollaris | South American painted-snipe |
| Haematopus palliatus | American oystercatcher |
| • Haematopus ater | Blackish oystercatcher |
| Haematopus leucopodus | Magellanic oystercatcher |
| • Vanellus chilensis | Southern lapwing |
| Charadrius falklandicus | Two-banded plover |
| • Charadrius modestus | Rufous-chested plover |
| Oreopholus ruficollis | Tawny-throated dotterel |
| Pluvianellus socialis | Magellanic plover |
| • Gallinago gallinago | Common snipe |
| Gallinago paraguaiae | South American (Paraguayan) snipe |
| Himantopus himantopus | Common stilt |
| Thinocorus rumicivorus | Least seedsnipe |
| Thinocorus orbignyianus | Gray-breasted seedsnipe |
| • Larus belcheri | Band-tailed gull |
| • Larus scoresbii | Dolphin gull |
| • Larus modestus | Grey gull |
| • Larus maculipennis | Brown-hooded gull |
| Sterna hirundinacea | South American tern |
| Sterna trudeaui | Snowy-crowned tern |
| Rynchops niger | Black skimmer |
| Cyanoliseus patagonus | Burrowing parrot |
| • Glaucidium brasilianum | Ferruginous pygmy-owl |
| • Zenaida auriculata | Eared dove |
| • Columbina picui | Picui ground-dove |
| Guira guira | *Guira cuckoo |
| Tapera naevia | Striped cuckoo |
| Coccyzus melacoryphus | Dark-billed cuckoo |
| Coccyzus cinereus | Ash-colored cuckoo |
| • Coccyzus euleri | Pearly-breasted cuckoo |
| • Crotophaga major | Greater ani |
| Crotophaga ani | Smooth-billed ani |
| Asio flammeus | *Short-eared owl |
| Lurocalis semitorquatus | Short-tailed nighthawk |
| Caprimulgus longirostris | Band-winged nightjar |
| Caprimulgus parvulus | Little nightjar |
| Podager nacunda | Nacunda nighthawk |
| Hydropsalis brasiliana | Scissor-tailed nightjar |
| Streptprocne zonaris | White-collared swift |
| Chaetura andrei | Ashy-tailed swift |
| • Cypseloides fumigatus | Sooty swift |
| • Anthracothorax nigricollis | Black-throated mango |
| • Patagona gigas | Giant hummingbird |
| Sephanoides sephaniodes | Green-backed firecrown |
| • Heliomaster furcifer | Blue-tufted starthroat |
| Calliphlox amethystina | Amethyst woodstar |
| Chlorostilbon aureoventris | Glittering-bellied emerald |
| Megaceryle torquata | Ringed kingfisher |
| • Picoides lignarius | Striped woodpecker |

# Passeriformes

| | |
|---|---|
| Geositta cunicularia | Common miner |
| Geositta antarctica | Short-billed miner |
| • Upucerthia dumetaria | Scale-throated earthcreeper |
| Cinclodes fuscus | Bar-winged cinclodes |
| • Cinclodes oustaleti | Grey-flanked cinclodes |
| • Cinclodes comechingonus | Cordoba cinclodes |
| Leptasthenura aegithaloides | Plain-mantled tit-spinetail |
| Phleocryptes melanops | Wren-like rushbird |
| Sparatonoica maluroides | *Bay-capped wren-spinetail |
| Synallaxis frontalis | Sooty-fronted spinetail |
| Synallaxis albescens | Pale-breasted spinetail |
| Crainoleuca sulphurifera | *Sulphur-bearded spinetail |
| Asthenes pyrrholeuca | Lesser (sharp-billed) canastero |
| Asthenes anthoides | Austral canastero |
| Asthenes hudsoni | *Hudson's canastero |
| • Phyllomyias burmeisteri | Rough-legged tyrannulet |
| • Phyllomyias fasciatus | Planalto tyrannulet |
| • Camptostoma obsoletum | Southern beardless-tyrannulet |
| • Phaeomyias murina | Mouse-colored tyrannulet |
| Inezia inornata | Plain tyrannulet |
| • Serpophaga subcristata | White-crested tryannulet |
| Serpophaga munda | White-bellied tyrannulet |
| • Serpophaga nigricans | Sooty tyrannulet |
| Suiriri suiriri | Chaco suiriri |
| Elaenia spectabilis | Large elaenia |
| Elaenia chiriquensis | Lesser elaenia |
| Elaenia albiceps | White-crested elaenia |
| Elaenia parvirostris | Small-billed elaenia |
| Elaenia strepera | Slaty elaenia |
| • Elaenia mesoleuca | Olivaceous elaenia |
| Sublegatus modestus | Southern scrub-flycatcher |
| Myiopagis viridicata | Greenish elaenia |
| • Myiopagis caniceps | Grey elaenia |
| Stigmatura budytoides | Greater wagtail-tyrant |
| Pseudocolopteryx flaviventris | Warbling doradito |
| Pseudocolopteryx acutipennis | Subtropical doradito |
| Pseudocolopteryx dinellianus | Dinelli's doradito |
| • Pseudocolopteryx sclateri | Crested doradito |
| • Euscarthmus meloryphus | Tawny-crowned pygmy-tyrant |
| Tachuris rubrigastra | Many-colored rush-tyrant |
| Polystictus pectoralis | Bearded tachuri |
| Anairetes parulus | Tufted tit-tyrant |
| Anairetes flavirostris | Yellow-billed tit-tyrant |
| Myiophobus fasciatus | Bran-colored flycatcher |
| • Contopus cinereus | Tropical pewee |
| Lathrotriccus euleri | Euler's flycatcher |
| Cnemotriccus fuscatus | Fuscous flycatcher |
| Pyrocephalus rubinus | Vermilion flycatcher |
| Colorhamphus parvirostris | Patagonian tyrant |
| Hirundinea ferruginea | Cliff flycatcher |
| Agriornis murina | Lesser shrike-tyrant |
| Agriornis montana | *Black-billed shrike-tyrant |
| Agriornis microptera | Gray-bellied shrike-tyrant |
| Agriornis livida | *Great shrike-tyrant |
| Muscisaxicola maculirostris | Spot-billed ground tyrant |
| Muscisaxicola cinerea | Cinereous ground-tyrant |
| Muscisaxicola albilora | White-browed ground-tyrant |
| Muscisaxicola rufivertex | *Rufous-naped ground-tyrant (altitudinal; austral?) |
| Muscisaxicola flavinucha | Ochre-naped ground-tyrant |
| Muscisaxicola frontalis | Black-fronted ground-tyrant |
| Muscisaxicola capistrata | Cinnamon-bellied ground-tyrant |
| Muscisaxicola macloviana | Dark-faced ground-tyrant |
| Neoxolmis rufiventris | Chocolate-vented tyrant |
| Neoxolmis rubetra | Rusty-backed monjita |
| Xolmis pyrope | Fire-eyed diucon |
| Xolmis cinerea | *Gray monjita |
| Xolmis coronata | Black-crowned monjita |
| Xolmis dominicana | *Black-and-white monjita |
| Heteroxolmis irupero | *White monjita |
| Satrapa icterophrys | Yellow-browed tyrant |

163

| | |
|---|---|
| • *Machetornis rixosus* | Cattle tyrant |
| *Knipolegus striaticeps* | Cinereous tyrant |
| *Knipolegus cyanirostris* | Blue-billed black-tyrant |
| *Knipolegus aterrimus* | White-winged black-tyrant |
| *Knipolegus hudsoni* | Hudson's black-tyrant |
| *Hymenops perspicillatus* | Spectacled tyrant |
| • *Fluvicola pica* | Pied-water tyrant |
| *Lessonia rufa* | Rufous-backed negrito |
| *Fluvicola albiventer* | Black-backed water-tyrant |
| *Alectrurus tricolor* | *Cock-tailed tyrant (nomadic?) |
| *Alectrurus risora* | Strange-tailed tyrant (nomadic?) |
| *Attila phoenicurus* | Rufous-tailed attila |
| *Casiornis rufa* | Rufous casiornis |
| *Myiarchus tyrannulus* | Brown-crested flycatcher |
| *Myiarchus swainsoni* | Swainson's flycatcher |
| *Myiarchus tuberculifer* | Dusky-capped flycatcher (only southernmost population?) |
| *Sirystes sibilator* | Sirystes (southern Brasil?) |
| *Pitangus sulphuratus* | Great kiskadee (central Argentina populations?) |
| • *Megarynchus pitangua* | Boat-billed flycatcher |
| *Myiozetetes similis* | Social flycatcher (movements mostly intratropical) |
| *Myiodynastes maculatus* | Streaked flycatcher |
| *Legatus leucophaius* | Piratic flycatcher |
| *Empidonomus varius* | Variegated flycatcher |
| *Griseotyrannus aurantioatrocristatus* | Crowned-slaty flycatcher |
| *Tyrannus albogularis* | White-throated kingbird (may not breed in austral region) |
| *Tyrannus savana* | Fork-tailed flycatcher |
| *Tyrannus melancholicus* | Tropical kingbird |
| • *Xenopsaris albinucha* | White-naped xenopsaris |
| *Pachyramphus polychopterus* | White-winged becard |
| *Pachyramphus validus* | Crested becard |
| • *Tityra cayana* | Black-tailed tityra |
| • *Procnias nudicollis* | Bare-throated bellbird |
| *Phytotoma rutila* | White-tipped plantcutter |
| *Phytotoma rara* | *Rufous-tipped plantcutter |
| *Phibalura flavirostris* | Swallow-tailed cotinga |
| *Progne tapera* | Brown-chested martin |
| *Progne chalybea* | Gray breasted martin |
| *Progne modesta* | Southern martin |
| *Tachycineta albiventer* | White-winged swallow |
| *Tachycineta leucorrhoa* | White-rumped swallow |
| *Tachycineta leucopyga* | Chilean swallow |
| *Notiochelidon cyanoleuca* | Blue-and-white swallow |
| *Stelgidopteryx ruficollis* | Southern rough-winged swallow |
| *Alopochelidon fucata* | Tawny-headed swallow |
| *Troglodytes aedon* | House wren |
| *Cistothorus platensis* | Grass wren (southernmost populations) |
| *Platycichla flavipes* | Yellow-legged thrush (or nomadic?) |
| *Turdus serranus* | *Glossy-black thrush (southernmost population?) |
| *Turdus chiguanco* | *Chiguanco thrush |
| *Turdus falcklandii* | Austral thrush |
| *Turdus fulviventris* | *Chestnut-bellied thrush |
| *Turdus amaurochalinus* | Creamy-bellied thrush |
| *Turdus leucomelas* | *Pale-breasted thrush |
| *Turdus nigriceps* | Andean slaty-thrush |
| *Turdus subularis* | Eastern slaty-thrush |
| *Mimus patagonicus* | Patagonian mockingbird |
| *Mimus triurus* | White-banded mockingbird |
| *Anthus furcatus* | *Short-billed pipit |
| *Anthus hellmayri* | Hellmayr's pipit |
| *Anthus correndera* | Correndera pipit |
| *Vireo olivaceous (or Vireo chivi)* | Red-eyed vireo (or chivi vireo) |
| • *Geothlypis aequinoctialis* | Masked yellowthroat |
| *Basileuterus leucoblepharus* | *White-rimmed (browed) warbler |
| *Dacnis cayana* | *Blue dacnis |
| *Tersina viridis* | Swallow tanager |
| *Thraupis palmarum* | *Palm tanager |
| *Thraupis sayaca* | *Sayaca tanager |

| | |
|---|---|
| • *Thraupis bonariensis* | Blue-and-yellow tanager |
| • *Tangara preciosa* | Chestnut-backed tanager |
| *Piranga flava* | Hepatic tanager |
| *Stephanophorus diadematus* | *Diademed tanager |
| • *Cyanoloxia glaucocaerulea* | Indigo grosbeak |
| • *Pheucticus aureoventris* | Black-backed grosbeak |
| • *Leistes superciliaris* | White-browed blackbird |
| *Sturnella loyca* | Long-tailed meadowlark |
| *Sturnella defilippii* | Pampas meadowlark (lesser red-breasted meadowlark) |
| *Pseudoleistes virescens* | *Brown-and-yellow marshbird |
| *Amblyramphus holosericeus* | *Scarlet-headed blackbird |
| *Agelaius ruficapillus* | *Chestnut-capped blackbird |
| *Agelaius cyanopus* | *Unicolored blackbird |
| *Agelaius thilius* | Yellow-winged blackbird |
| *Curaeus curaeus* | *Austral blackbird |
| *Molothrus bonariensis* | *Shiny cowbird |
| *Molothrus badius* | *Bay-winged cowbird |
| *Cacicus solitarius* | *Solitary (solitary black) cacique |
| *Cacicus chrysopterus* | *Golden-winged cacique |
| • *Volatinia jacarina* | Blue-black grassquit |
| *Sporophila lineola* | Lined seedeater |
| *Sporophila caerulescens* | Double-collared seedeater |
| • *Sporophila melanogaster* | Black-bellied seedeater |
| *Sporophila leucoptera* | *White-bellied seedeater |
| *Sporophila bouvreuil* | Capped seedeater (nomadic?) |
| *Sporophila hypoxantha* | Tawny-bellied seedeater |
| • *Sporophila zelichi* | Narosky's seedeater |
| *Sporophila castaneiventris* | Chestnut-bellied seedeater |
| *Sporophila cinnamomea* | Chestnut seedeater |
| *Sporophila palustris* | Marsh seedeater |
| *Sporophila ruficollis* | Dark-throated seedeater (nomadic?) |
| • *Catamenia analis* | Band-tailed seedeater |
| • *Melanodera xanthogramma* | Yellow-bridled finch |
| *Phrygilus unicolor* | *Plumbeous sierra-finch |
| *Phrygilus plebejus* | Ash-breasted sierra-finch |
| *Phrygilus fruticeti* | Mourning sierra-finch |
| *Phrygilus carbonarius* | Carbonated sierra-finch |
| *Phrygilus gayi* | Gray-hooded sierra-finch |
| *Phrygilus patagonicus* | Patagonian sierra-finch |
| *Diuca diuca* | Common Diuca-finch |
| *Poospiza torquata* | Ringed warbling-finch |
| *Poospiza ornata* | Cinnamon warbling-finch |
| *Poospiza nigrorufa* | *Black-and-rufous warbling-finch |
| *Zonotrichia capensis* | Rufous-collared sparrow |
| *Ammodramus humeralis* | *Grassland sparrow |
| *Donacospiza albifrons* | *Long-tailed reed-finch |
| *Sicalis citrina* | *Stripe-tailed yellow-finch |
| *Sicalis luteola* | Grassland yellow-finch |
| • *Sicalis auriventris* | Greater yellow-finch |
| • *Sicalis olivascens* | Greenish yellow-finch |
| *Sicalis lebruni* | Patagonian yellow-finch |
| *Spinus barbatus* | Black-chinned siskin (at least local movements) |
| *Carduelis uropygialis* | Yellow-rumped siskin |

# LITERATURE CITED AND CONSULTED

American Ornithologists' Union. 1983. *Checklist of North American birds, 6th Edition.* AOU.

Andrade, G.I. (ed.) 1993. *Carpanta: selva nublada y paramo.* Fundación Natura. Colombia.

Arribas, M.A., Jammes, L., and F. Sagot. 1995. *Lista de las aves de Bolivia.* Asociación Armonía. Bolivia.

Askins, R.A. 1995. Hostile landscapes and the decline of migratory songbirds. Science 267: 1956-1957.

Bailey, R.G. 1983. Delineation of ecosystem regions. Environmental Management 7: 365-373.

Bailey, R.G. 1989a. Ecoregions of the continents. (Map.) U.S. Department of Agriculture, Forest Service. Washington, D.C.

Bailey, R.G. 1989b. Explanatory supplement to the ecoregions map of the continents. Environmental Conservation 15(4): 307-309.

Bailey, Robert G. 1996. *Ecosystem geography.* Springer. New York, New York.

Barlow, J.C. 1980. Patterns of ecological interactions among migrant and resident vireos on the wintering grounds. Pages 79-107 in Keast, A.K. and E.S. Morton (eds.). *Migrant birds in the neotropics: Ecology, behavior, distribution, and conservation.* Smithsonian Institution Press. Washington, D.C.

Barnes, B.V., Pregitzer, K.S., Spies, T.A., and V.H. Spooner. 1982. Ecological forest site classification. Journal of Forestry 80: 493-498.

Barnes, B.V. 1984. Forest ecosystem classification and mapping in Baden-Wurtemberg, West Germany. In: *Forest land classification: Experience, problems, perspectives. Proceedings of the symposium, March 18-20.* Madison, Wisconsin.

Best, B. J. and M. Kessler. 1995. *Biodiversity and conservation in Tumbesian Ecuador and Peru.* Birdlife International. United Kingdom.

Blake, J.G. and B.A. Loiselle. 1989. Habitat use by neotropical migrants at La Selva Biological Station and Braulio Carrillo National Park, Costa Rica. Pages 257-272 in Hagan III, J.M. and D.W. Johnston (eds.). *Ecology and conservation of neotropical migrant landbirds.* Smithsonian Institution Press. Washington, D.C.

Carillo, N. and J. Icochea. 1995. Lista taxonómica de los reptiles vivientes del Perú. Publ. Mus. Hist. Natural UNMSM (A) 49: 1-27. Lima, Peru.

Chesser, R.T. 1994. *Migration in South America: An overview of the austral system.* Bird Conservation International 4: 91-107.

Davis, S.E. 1989. Migration of the Mississippi kite *Ictinia mississippiensis* in Bolivia, with comments on *I. plumbea.* Bull. B.O.C. 109(3): 149-152.

Dietz, J. M., Dietz, L.A., and E.Y. Nagagata. 1994. The effective use of flagship species for conservation of biodiversity: The example of lion tamarins in Brazil. Pages 32-49 in Olney, P.J.S., Mace, G. M., and A. T. C. Feistner (eds.). *Creative conservation: Interactive management of wild and captive animals.* Chapman and Hall. London.

Dinerstein, E., Olson, D.M., Graham, D.J., Webster, A.L., Primm, S.A., Bookbinder, M.P., and G. Ledec. 1995. *A conservation assessment of the terrestrial ecoregions of Latin America and the Caribbean.* The World Bank. Washington, D.C.

Dlouhy, C.J. and C.L. Weber. 1991. Checklist of birds of Paraguay (exact title unavailable). Natural History Museum of Geneva.

Driscoll, R.S., Merkel, D.L., Radloff, D.L., Snyder, D.E., and J.S. Hagihara . 1984. An ecological land classification framework for the United States. Miscellaneous Publication 1439. U.S. Department of Agriculture, Forest Service. Washington, D.C.

Finch, D.M. 1991. Population ecology, habitat requirements, and conservation of neotropical migratory birds. USDA Forest Service General Tech. Report RM-205.

Fitzpatrick, J.W. 1980. Wintering of North American tyrant flycatchers in the neotropics. Pages 67-78 in Keast, A.K. and E.S. Morton (eds.). *Migrant birds in the neotropics: Ecology, behavior, distribution, and conservation.* Smithsonian Institution Press. Washington, D.C.

Fjeldsa, J. and Krabbe, N. 1990. *Birds of the high Andes.* Zoological Museum, University of Copenhagen, Copenhagen.

Fundación Natura. 1992. *Diagnóstico socioeconómico de la Reserva Ecológica Cayambe/Coca: Estudios en areas protegidas 2.* Quito, Ecuador.

Gallant, A.L., Whittier, T.R., Larsen, D.P., Omernik, J.M., and R.M. Hughes. 1989. Regionalization as a tool for managing environmental recources. U.S. Environmental Protection Agency. EPA/600/3-89/060. Corvalis, Oregon.

Gill, F. 1990. *Ornithology.* W.H. Freeman & Co. New York, New York.

Greenberg, R. 1989a. Forest migrants in non-forest habitats on the Yucatan Peninsula. Pages 273-286 in Hagan III, J.M. and D.W. Johnston (eds.). *Ecology and conservation of neotropical migrant landbirds.* Smithsonian Institution Press. Washington, D.C.

Greenberg, R. 1989b. The nonbreeding season: Introduction. Pages 175-177 in Hagan III, J.M. and D.W. Johnston (eds.). *Ecology and conservation of neotropical migrant landbirds.* Smithsonian Institution Press. Washington, D.C.

Haffer, J. 1974. Avian speciation in tropical South America. Publication of the Nuttall Ornithological Club, No. 14. Nuttall Ornithological Club. Cambridge, Massachusetts.

Harris, M. 1982. *A field guide to the birds of Galapagos.* Collins. St. James Place, London.

Hayes, F.E., Goodman, S.M., Fox, J.A., Tamayo, T.G., and N. López. 1992. North American bird migrants in Paraguay. The Condor 92: 947-960.

Hayes, F.E. 1995a. Definitions for migrant birds: What is a neotropical migrant? Accepted 27 January 1995 for publication in The Auk.

Hayes, F.E. 1995b. Status, distribution, and biogeography of the birds of Paraguay. Monogr. Field Ornithol. 1: 1-224. American Birding Association. Colorado Springs, Colorado.

Hills, G.A. 1952. The classification of and evaluation of sites for forestry. Ontario Department of Lands and Forests. Resource Division Report 24.

Hilty, S.L. 1980. Relative abundance of north temperate zone breeding migrants in western Colombia and their impact at fruiting trees. Pages 265-271 in Keast, A.K. and E.S. Morton (eds.). *Migrant birds in the neotropics: Ecology, behavior, distribution, and conservation.* Smithsonian Institution Press. Washington, D.C.

Hilty, S.L. and W.L. Brown. 1986. *A guide to the birds of Colombia.* Princeton University Press. Princeton, New Jersey.

Holdridge, L.R. 1967. *Life zone ecology.* Tropical Science Center. San Jose, California.

Holmes, R.T. and T. W. Sherry. 1989. Site fidelity of migratory warblers in temperate breeding and neotropical wintering areas: Implications for population dynamics, habitat selection, and conservation. Pages 563-578 in Hagan III, J.M. and D.W. Johnston (eds.). *Ecology and conservation of neotropical migrant landbirds.* Smithsonian Institution Press. Washington, D.C.

Hunter, W.C. 1995. Unpublished data. Partners in Flight Neotropical Migratory Bird Program (ultimately data will be part of Colorado Bird Observatory Partners in Flight Database).

Hunter, W.C., Carter, M.F., Pashley, D.N., and K. Barker. 1993. The partners in flight species prioritization scheme. Pages 109-119 in Finch, D.M and P.W. Stangel (eds.). *Status and management of neotropical migratory birds.* Proc. USDA Forest Service, RM-229. Fort Collins, Colorado.

Hunter, W.C. and D. N. Pashley. 1995. Unpublished Partners in Flight concern scores.

Hutto, R.L. 1989. Habitat distributions of migratory landbird species in western Mexico. Pages 211-239 in Hagan III, J.M. and D.W. Johnston (eds.). *Ecology and conservation of neotropical migrant landbirds.* Smithsonian Institution Press. Washington, D.C.

International Council for Bird Preservation. 1981. *Endangered birds of the world: The ICBP bird red data book.* Smithsonian Institution Press. Washington, D.C.

International Council for Bird Preservation. 1992. *Putting biodiversity on the map: Priority areas for global conservation.* International Council for Bird Preservation. Cambridge, United Kingdom.

International Council for Bird Preservation/The World Conservation Union. 1992. *Threatened birds of the Americas: The ICBP/IUCN red data book.* Smithsonian Institution Press. Washington, D.C.

Isler, M.L. and P.R. Isler. 1987. *The tanagers: Natural history, distribution, and identification.* Smithsonian Institution Press. Washington, D.C.

IUCN 1994. *1993 United Nations list of national parks and protected areas.* Prepared by WCMC and CNPPA. IUSN. Gland, Switzerland and Cambridge, United Kingdom.

James, F.C., McCulloch, C.E., and D.A. Wiedenfeld. 1996. New approaches to the analysis of population trends in land birds. Ecology 77(1): 13-27.

Johnson, T.B. 1980. Resident and North American migrant bird interactions in the Santa Marta highlands, northern Colombia. Pages 239-247 in Keast, A.K. and E.S. Morton (eds.). *Migrant birds in the neotropics: Ecology, behavior, distribution, and conservation.* Smithsonian Institution Press. Washington, D.C.

Jones, R.K., Pierpoint, G., and G.M. Wickware. 1983. Field guide to forest ecosystem classification for the clay belt, site region 3e. Ministry of Natural Resources. Ontario, Canada.

Keast, A. 1980. Spatial relationships between migratory parulid warblers and their ecological counterparts in the neotropics. Pages 109-130 in Keast, A.K. and E.S. Morton. (eds.). *Migrant birds in the neotropics: Ecology, behavior, distribution, and conservation.* Smithsonian Institution Press. Washington, D.C.

Kerlinger, P. 1992. Birding economics and birder demographics studies as conservation tools. Pages 32-38 in Finch, D.M and P.W. Stangel (eds.). *Status and management of neotropical migratory birds.* Proc. USDA Forest Service, RM-229. Fort Collins, Colorado.

Kricher, J.C. and W.E. Davis. 1989. Patterns of avian species richness in disturbed and undisturbed habitats in Belize. Pages 240-246 in Hagan III, J.M. and D.W. Johnston (eds.). *Ecology and conservation of neotropical migrant landbirds.* Smithsonian Institution Press. Washington, D.C.

Lynch, J.F. 1989. Distribution of overwintering nearctic migrants in the Yucatan Peninsula, of native and human-modified vegetation. Pages 178-196 in Hagan III, J.M. and D.W. Johnston (eds.). *Ecology and conservation of neotropical migrant landbirds.* Smithsonian Institution Press. Washington, D.C.

Mabey, S.E. and E.S. Morton. 1989. Demography and territorial behavior of wintering Kentucky warblers in Panama. Pages 329-336 in Hagan III, J.M. and D.W. Johnston (eds.). *Ecology and conservation of neotropical migrant landbirds.* Smithsonian Institution Press. Washington, D.C.

Mayer, S. 1992. Birds observed in and near the reserve of Tariquia, dpto. Tarija, Bolivia, in September/October. Unpublished. The Netherlands.

Meyer de Schauensee, R. and W.H. Phelps Jr. 1978. *A guide to the birds of Venezuela.* Princeton Univ. Press. Princeton, New Jersey.

Meyer de Schauensee, R. and W. H. Phelps Jr. 1994. *Una guía de las aves de Venezuela.* Suplemento. Princeton Univ. Press. Princeton, New Jersey.

Moore, F.R. and T.R. Simons. 1989. Habitat suitability and stopover ecology of neotropical landbird migrants. Pages 345-355 in Hagan III, J.M. and D.W. Johnston (eds.). *Ecology and conservation of neotropical migrant landbirds.* Smithsonian Institution Press, Washington, D.C.

Morrison, R.I.G. and R. K. Ross. 1989a. *Atlas of nearctic shorebirds on the coast of South America.* Vol. 1. Canadian Wildlife Service Special Publication. Canada.

Morrison, R.I.G. and R.K. Ross. 1989b. *Atlas of nearctic shorebirds on the coast of South America.* Vol. 2. Canadian Wildlife Service Special Publication. Canada.

Morton, E.S. 1980. Adaptations to seasonal changes by migrant land birds in the Panama Canal zone. Pages 109-130 in Keast, A.K. and E.S. Morton (eds.) *Migrant birds in the neotropics: Ecology, behavior, distribution, and conservation.* Smithsonian Institution Press. Washington, D.C.

Morton, E.S. 1989. What do we know about the future of migrant landbirds? Pages 579-589 in Hagan III, J.M. and D.W. Johnston (eds.). *Ecology and conservation of neotropical migrant landbirds.* Smithsonian Institution Press. Washington, D.C.

Noss, R.F. and R.L. Peters. 1995. *Endangered ecosystems: A status report on America's vanishing habitat and wildlife.* Defenders of Wildlife. Washington, D.C.

O'Connor, R.J. 1989. Population variation in relation to migrancy status in some North American birds. Pages 64-74 in Hagan III, J.M. and D.W. Johnston (eds.). *Ecology and conservation of neotropical migrant landbirds.* Smithsonian Institution Press, Washington, D.C.

Omernick, J.M. 1987. Ecoregions of the conterminous United States. Annals of the Association of American Geographers 77: 118-125.

Ortiz, F., Greenfield, P., and J.C. Matheus. 1990. *Aves del Ecuador.* Fundación Ecuatoriana de Promocion Turistica Feprotur and Corporacion Ornitologica del Ecuador, Ecuador.

Pacheco, V., de Macedo, H., Vivar, E., Ascorra, C., Arana-Cardó, R., and S. Solari. 1995. Lista anotada de los mamíferos peruanos. Conservation International. Occasional Paper No.2.

Parker III, T.A., Parker, S.A., and M.A. Plenge. 1982. *An annotated checklist of Peruvian birds.* North Central Publishing Co. St. Paul, Minnesota.

Pearson, D.L. 1980. Bird migration in Amazonian Ecuador, Peru, and Bolivia. Pages 273-283 in Keast, A.K. and E.S. Morton (eds.). *Migrant birds in the neotropics: Ecology, behavior, distribution, and conservation.* Smithsonian Institution Press. Washington, D.C.

Pough, S.H., Heiser, J.B., and W.N. MacFarland. 1989. *Vertebrate life.* McMillan Publishing Co. New York, New York.

Price, J., Droge, S., and A. Price. 1995. *The summer atlas of North American birds.* Academic Press. San Diego, California.

Rappole, J.H. 1995. *The ecology of migrant birds: A neotropical perspective.* Smithsonian Institution Press. Washington, D.C.

Rappole, J.H., Morton, E.S., and M.A. Ramos. 1989. Density, philopatry, and population estimates for songbird migrants wintering in Veracruz. Pages 337-344 in Hagan III, J.M. and D.W. Johnston (eds.). *Ecology and conservation of neotropical migrant landbirds.* Smithsonian Institution Press, Washington, D.C.

Rappole, J.H., Morton, E.S., Lovejoy III, T.E., and J.L. Ruos. 1995. *Nearctic avian migrants in the neotropics: Maps, appendices, and bibliography.* Second edition. Smithsonian Institution Press. Washington, D.C.

Rasmussen, J.F., Rahbek, C., Horstman, E., Poulsen, M.K., and H. Bloch. 1994. *Aves del parque nacional Podocarpus: Una lista anotada.* Corporacion Ornitologica del Ecuador. Ecuador.

Reed, J.M. 1989. A system for ranking conservation priorities for neotropical migrant birds based on relative susceptibility to extinction. Pages 524-536 in Hagan III, J.M. and D.W. Johnston (eds.). *Ecology and conservation of neotropical migrant landbirds.* Smithsonian Institution Press. Washington, D.C.

Ridgely, R.S. 1995. Set of unpublished range maps. The Academy of Natural Sciences. Philadelphia, Pennsylvania.

Ridgely, R. S. and G. Tudor. 1989. *The birds of South America*. Vol. 1. Univ. Texas Press. Austin, Texas.

Ridgely, R. S. and G. Tudor. 1994. *The birds of South America*. Vol. 2. Univ. Texas Press. Austin, Texas.

Robbins, C.S., Dowell, B.A., Dawson, D.K., Colón, J.A., Estrada, R., Sutton, A., Sutton, R., and D. Weyer. 1989a. Comparison of neotropical migrant landbird populations wintering in tropical forest, isolated fragments, and agricultural habitats. Pages 207-220 in Hagan III, J.M. and D.W. Johnston (eds.). *Ecology and conservation of neotropical migrant landbirds*. Smithsonian Institution Press. Washington, D.C.

Robbins, C.S, Fitzpatrick, J.W., and P.B. Hamel. 1989b. A warbler in trouble: Dendroica cerulea. Pages 549-562 in Hagan III, J.M. and D.W. Johnston (eds.). *Ecology and conservation of neotropical migrant landbirds*. Smithsonian Institution Press. Washington, D.C.

Robbins, C.S., Sauer, J.R., Greenberg, R.S., and S. Droege. 1989c. Population declines in North American birds that migrate to the neotropics. Proc. Natl. Acad. Sci. 86: 7658-7662.

Robinson, S.K., Fitzpatrick, J.W., and J. Terborgh. 1995a. *Distribution and habitat use of neotropical migrant landbirds in the Amazon basin and Andes*. Bird Conservation International 5: 305-323.

Robinson, S.K., Thompson III, F.R., Donovan, T.M., Whitehead, D.R., and J. Faaborg. 1995b. Regional forest fragmentation and the nesting success of migratory birds. Science 267: 1987-1989.

Rodríguez, L., Córdova, J., and J. Icochea. 1993. Lista preliminar de los anfibios del Perú. Publ. Mus. Hist. Natural UNMSM (A) 45: 1-22.

Sauer, J.R. and S. Droege (eds.). 1990. Survey designs and statistical methods for the estimation of avian population trends. FWS. Biol. Rep. 90(1). Washington, D.C.

Shaw, D. and T.C. Maxwell. 1990. First record of the Mississippi kite for Bolivia. J. Raptor Res. 22(3): 90.

Sherry, T.W. and R.T Holmes. 1992. Are populations of neotropical migrant birds limited in summer or winter? Implications for management. Pages 47-57 in Finch, D.M. and P.W. Stangel (eds.). *Status and management of neotropical migratory birds*. Proc. USDA Forest Service, RM-229. Fort Collins, Colorado.

Sibley, C.G. and B.L. Monroe Jr. 1990. Distribution and taxonomy of birds of the world. Yale University Press. New Haven, Connecticut.

Smith, N.G. 1980. Hawk and vulture migrations in the neotropics. Pages 51-65 in Keast, A.K. and E.S. Morton (eds.). *Migrant birds in the neotropics: Ecology, behavior, distribution, and conservation*. Smithsonian Institution Press. Washington, D.C.

Staicer, C.A. 1989. Social behavior of the northern parula, Cape May warbler, and prairie warbler wintering in second-growth forest in southwestern Puerto Rico. Pages 308-320 in Hagan III, J.M. and D.W. Johnston (eds.). *Ecology and conservation of neotropical migrant landbirds*. Smithsonian Institution Press. Washington, D.C.

Terborgh, J. 1989a. Perspectives on the conservation of neotropical migrant landbirds. Pages 7-12 in Hagan III, J.M. and D.W. Johnston (eds.). *Ecology and conservation of neotropical migrant landbirds*. Smithsonian Institution Press. Washington, D.C.

Terborgh, J. 1989b. *Where have all the birds gone?* Princeton Univ. Press. Princeton, New Jersey.

Terborgh, J., Robinson, S.K., Parker III, T.A., Munn, C.A., and N. Pierpont. 1990. Structure and organization of an Amazonian forest bird community. Ecolog. Monog. 60(2): 213-238.

Terres, J.K. 1993. *The Audubon Society encyclopedia of North American birds*. Random House. New York, New York.

The Nature Conservancy, Conservation Science Division, in association with the Network of Natural Heritage Programs and Conservation Data Centers. March 1995a. Element National Ranking Database. Arlington, Virginia.

The Nature Conservancy. 1995b. *Parks in peril source book*. The Nature Conservancy, Latin America and Caribbean Division. Arlington, Virginia.

Turkel, T. 1992. Fading songs of spring. Maine Sunday Telegram. May 17.

Udvardy, M.D.F. 1975. A classification of the biogeographical provinces of the world. International Union for Conservation of Nature and Natural Resources. Occasional Paper 18. Morges, Switzerland.

United States Fish and Wildlife Service. 1990. Conservation of avian diversity in North America. Prepared by the Office of Migratory Bird Management.

United States Naval Hydrographic Office. 1968. Sailing directions, South American pilot. Vol. III. Comprising the western coast of South America. 5th edition. Hydrographic Office Publ.

Vasquez, P. 1995. Unpublished data. CDC Universidad Nacional Agraria la Molina. Peru.

Walter, H. and E. Box. 1976. Global classification of natural terrestrial ecosystems. Vegetatio 32: 75-81.

Wege, D.C. and A.J. Long. 1995. *Key areas for birds in the neotropics*. Birdlife International. United Kingdom.

Wertz, W.A. and J.A. Arnold. 1972. Land Systems Inventory. USDA Forest Service, Intermountain Region. Ogden, Utah.

Wiken, E.B. (compiler). 1986. Terrestrial ecozones of Canada. Ecological Land Classification Series No. 19. Hull, PQ: Environment Canada. Hull.

Wille, C. 1994. The birds and the beans. Audubon 96(6): 58-64.

Winker, K., Warner, D.W., and A.R. Weisbrod. 1989. The northern waterthrush and Swainson's thrush as transients at a temperate inland stopover site. Pages 384-402 in Hagan III, J.M. and D.W. Johnston (eds.). *Ecology and conservation of neotropical migrant landbirds.* Smithsonian Institution Press. Washington, D.C.

World Resources Institute. 1994. World Resources 1994-95. Oxford University Press. Oxford.

Zalles, J.I. and K.L. Bildstein, eds. 1995. *Manual de observatorios de migración de rapaces.* Hawk Mountain Sanctuary Association. Kempton, Pennsylvania.

# ENDNOTES

Refer to the Literature Cited and Consulted section for complete citations of published sources.

[1] Robbins *et al.* 1989c, pp. 7658-7661.

[2] Ecoregion classification schemes have been developed for geographical scales ranging from global to local. For a climatic and vegetation approach at a global scale, see Holdridge (1967), Walter and Box (1976), Udvardy (1975), Bailey (1983, 1989b, and 1996). Bailey (1983) suggested that his hierarchical system could be extended to regional and local scales by applying land stratification concepts of Wertz and Arnold (1972). Other ecoregion classification schemes are based on regional scales: see Driscoll *et al.* (1984), Gallant *et al.* (1989), Omernik (1987) in the United States, and Wiken (1986) in Canada. Still others are based on subregional to local scales. In the United States, see Barnes *et al.* (1982). In Canada, see Jones *et al.* (1983) and Hills (1952). In Germany, see Barnes (1984).

[3] See *A Conservation Assessment of the Terrestrial Ecoregions of Latin America and the Caribbean* (Dinerstein *et al.* 1995). This study was financed by the World Bank, Global Environment Facility, and the World Wildlife Fund.

[4] Dinerstein *et al.* 1995, p. 4.

[5] The variety of habitats existing within an ecoregion may be used differentially by bird species. A species may occur in one portion of an ecoregion and not another. Further, it should be noted that the names given ecoregions may not reflect all of the habitats that occur within that ecoregion. Consequently, an ecoregion's name may not describe a species' typical habitat preferences even though that bird inhabits portions of that ecoregion. An example is the Ecuadorian dry forest ecoregion, which encompasses the Machalilla National Park in Ecuador. Many shorebirds occur in this park, but obviously are not thought of as inhabiting "dry forest." Another example is the Sechura desert, which has a high species richness due to its coastal position. A large number of shorebird species are present despite the desert habitat.

[6] Kerlinger 1992, p. 32.

[7] Dietz *et al.* 1994, pp. 32-49.

[8] Our working definition of neotropical migratory birds is framed by national boundaries, which inevitably influence conservation. The strict definition would include all avian species that migrate to the neotropics. Rappole et al. (1995) include "at least" 338 species on their list of nearctic migrants, defined as "any western hemisphere species, all or part of whose populations breed north of the Tropic of Cancer and winter south of that line." Rappole et al. (1995) mentions another 80 to 90 species that breed in the subtropics of southern Texas, Arizona, New Mexico, and northern Mexico and migrate into the tropics; many of these are included in our list of 406 neotropical migrants because they breed in the United States but migrate south of the border to varying degrees.

[9] It should be noted that the variance in a given population estimate cannot be adequately calculated when the estimate is based on less than 14 routes at the state level or less than 50 routes at the national level, and the North American Breeding Bird Survey suggests using caution when assessing trends derived from these estimates. For the purposes of this project, however, all negative trends were compiled, regardless of the number of routes. It should be noted also that the survey's trends do not exist for all of the selected

neotropical migrants to the ASC Region. Because of the limitations of road counts, trends are generally unavailable for seabirds and shorebirds.

[10] James *et al.* 1996. pp. 13-27.

[11] Hunter *et al.* 1993, p. 109.

[12] Hunter and Pashley, unpublished data, 1995. Partners in Flight concern scores were derived from this dataset.

[13] Our list of species with a South American affinity represents a combination and enhancement of several previous efforts by others, including Terborgh (1989b) and Hunter (unpublished). It is important to note that the list is likely to change as new data become available on the distribution and abundance of neotropical migrants throughout Latin America.

[14] Even if reliable data on transient versus resident preferences were generally available, its value to this kind of study is questionable because there is currently no way to determine the relative importance of nonbreeding versus stopover habitats. A given habitat along the migratory routes could be an essential visual marker during migration or a place where a bird briefly forages and not be documented as yet. "The fact that migrants need to refuel at frequent intervals, that they often become concentrated into particular flyways and stopover points, and that some at least are territorial in passage habitats, indicate the potential importance of suitable stopover habitats." (Turkel 1992)

[15] The World Bank-World Wildlife Fund ecoregion classification scheme is currently limited to terrestrial areas. In order to assess the distribution and status of birds that use certain aquatic habitats, we clarified national boundaries for mangrove areas identified by Dinerstein *et al.* (1995), created an additional ecoregion for the Venezuelan islands, and designated pelagic zones to supplement the World Bank-World Wildlife Fund scheme. Additionally, we assembled the geographic coverage of Parks in Peril sites primarily through in-house digitizing of maps provided by Latin American partners as well as through use of a pre-existing map of protected areas developed by the World Conservation Monitoring Center.

[16] As previously noted, ecoregions are not homogeneous for habitat types, and thus the distribution of a bird species occurring in a given ecoregion will not be uniform. One ecoregion can include an array of habitats of varying usefulness to birds, most of which are not indicated by the ecoregion's name. It is also important to remember that ecoregions are based on historical extent and that vast portions of certain ecoregions may no longer exist in their original condition. For example, aquatic habitats (rivers, lakes, ponds, lagoons, marshes, rocky shores, sandy shores), pastures (grassy areas), agricultural fields (rice and other crops), urban areas (cities, gardens), plantations (cocoa, coffee, orange), and secondary woodlands exist in many of the ecoregions and are used differentially by various species.

[17] Despite our effort to acquire the best information on the occurrence and habitat selection of neotropical migratory birds in the ASC Region, there are gaps in the information that can be filled only through data acquired from new sources such as field studies. For example, our assumption that a species occurs in a Parks in Peril site if it is thought to occur in similar habitat elsewhere in an overlapping ecoregion may lead to occasional over-estimation of species lists for Parks in Peril sites. In addition, birds have not been studied adequately in large areas of South America. Many species probably occur in places where they have not been recorded as yet. A good example of this situation is the Macarena montane forests in Colombia. Finally, difficulty in distinguishing migrants from year-round residents in a given area for species that have a dual migrant and resident status increases the uncertainty in assessing the distribution of neotropical migratory birds.

[18] Ridgely and Tudor 1989, p. 3. The total known species of birds on the planet is 9,672. See Sibley and Monroe 1990.

[19] Greenberg 1989b, p. 175.

[20] Rappole 1995. Under Rappole's theory the timing, routes, and triggering mechanisms for this migration became modified by natural selection over generations, resulting in the survival of birds that are successful in exploiting seasonally abundant food resources in the temperate zone. This theory is supported by various lines of evidence, including taxonomic relationships among nearctic migrants, some recent examples of the rapid development of long-distance migration, and new evidence that migrations are part of the life history for many species of neotropical resident birds.

[21] Morrison and Ross 1989b, p. 281.

[22] U.S. Naval Hydrographic Office 1968. Cited in Morrison and Ross 1989b, p. 281.

[23] Robinson et al. 1995, p. 305. Robinson et al. found that most of the 30 species of northern migrants that regularly winter in South America appear to be concentrated in the western edge of the Amazon basin and on the lower slopes of the Andes.

[24] Rappole 1995, pp. 142-143 and 162-163. The broad-winged hawk, Swainson's hawk, upland sandpiper, and barn swallow are among the species that show significant population declines in various surveys (not limited to the BBS long-term trends). The American golden plover and the yellow-green vireo are among the species that Rappole considers most likely to decline in the near future.

[25] Haffer 1974.

[26] Wege and Long 1995. Birdlife International established these designations by mapping the overlapping distributions of birds that in historical times have had breeding ranges of less than 50,000 square kilometers and by identifying those areas in which two or more of these restricted-range birds are totally confined in close geographic proximity. We found that the ecoregions with the most Endemic Bird Areas within their boundaries are the northwestern Andean montane forests, eastern Cordillera Real montane forests, and the Peruvian yungas, each containing a total of four Endemic Bird Areas. Those ecoregions with three Endemic Bird Areas existing within their boundaries are the Cordillera Central paramo, Ucayli moist forests, and the northern Andean paramo. The cool and fairly barren paramos are typically species-poor, and the unexpectedly high number of Endemic Bird Areas within the World Bank-World Wildlife Fund paramo ecoregions is most likely caused by the disagreement over geographic locations of paramos between the World Bank-World Wildlife Fund ecoregion maps and Birdlife International's Endemic Bird Area maps. All of the remaining ecoregions in the ASC Region contain either two, one, or zero Endemic Bird Areas within their boundaries. It should be noted that there are relatively few Endemic Bird Areas designated in the Amazonian basin because the species of this region are widely distributed. Also, the distributions of Amazonian birds are generally not well known, so the boundaries of Endemic Bird Areas in this region are approximated (ICBP 1992).

[27] Ridgely and Tudor 1989, p. 25.

[28] *Ibid.*

[29] Ridgely and Tudor 1989, cited in ICBP 1992, p. 30.

[30] Wege and Long 1995, p. 18.

[31] *Ibid.* These include the eastern Cordillera Real montane forests, northwestern Andean montane forests, Chocó/Darién moist forests, mangroves of Colombia, Ecuadorian dry forests, Tumbes/Piura dry forests, Guayaquil flooded grasslands, mangroves of Ecuador and Peru, Sechura desert, northwestern Andean montane forests, and the western Ecuador moist forest.

[32] TNC 1995b, p. 81.

[33] IUCN 1994, p. 30.

[34] Arribas *et al.* 1995.

[35] Ridgely and Tudor 1989, p. 25.

[36] Dinerstein *et al.* 1995, pp. 90-99.

[37] According to Tyler (1942) and Terres (1958), cited in Terres 1993, p. 389.

[38] TNC 1995b, p. 88.

[39] Hilty and Brown 1986, p. 3.

[40] IUCN 1994, p. 68.

[41] Hilty and Brown 1986, p. 32.

[42] Dinerstein *et al.* 1995, p. 91.

[43] Ridgely and Tudor 1989, p. 25.

[44] Dinerstein *et al.* 1995, p. 89.

[45] Hilty and Brown 1986, p. 27.

[46] Ridgely and Tudor 1989, p. 168.

[47] TNC 1995b, p. 102.

[48] Ortiz *et al.* 1990, introduction.

[49] TNC 1995b, p. 106.

[50] IUCN 1994, p. 78.

[51] Ridgely pers. comm. 1996.

[52] Dinerstein *et al.* 1995, p. 95.

[53] Ridgely and Tudor 1989. p. 25.

[54] Dinerstein *et al.* 1995, p. 92.

[55] Ridgely pers. comm. 1995. These islands are off the main flyways, and many of the species reported are vagrants.

[56] Harris 1982, p. 32.

[57] TNC internal document.

[58] Fundación Natura 1992, p. 40.

[59] TNC internal document.

[60] *Ibid.*

[61] TNC 1995b, p. 111.

[62] Hayes 1995b.

[63] Dinerstein *et al.* 1995, p. 99.

[64] *Ibid.*

[65] Madroño pers. comm. 1995.

[66] IUCN 1994, p. 154.

[67] TNC 1995b, p. 116.

[68] Vasquez pers. comm. 1995. Citing Pacheco et al. 1995; Rodriguez, Cordoba and Icochea 1993; and Carillo and Icochea 1995.

[69] IUCN 1994, p. 155.

[70] Vasquez pers. comm. 1995.

[71] Dinerstein *et al.* 1995, p. 92.

[72] *Ibid.,* p. 90.

[73] TNC 1995b, p. 122.

[74] Meyer de Schauensee and Phelps 1994 (supplement).

[75] IUCN 1994, p. 237.

[76] Dinerstein *et al.* 1995, p. 88.

[77] Ridgely pers. comm. These islands are, for the most part, stepping stones for migrants on their way to the South American continent after flying across the Caribbean.

[78] Meyer de Schauensee and Phelps 1978, p. 356.

[79] Dinerstein et al. 1995, p. 98.

[80] Ridgely and Tudor 1989, p. 19.

[81] Dinerstein *et al.* 1995, p. 88.

[82] See Introduction, p. x.

[83] Rappole 1995, p. 136.

[84] Finch 1991, p. 1.

[85] Noss and Peters 1995, p. viii.

[86] Askins 1995, p. 1956.

[87] Price *et al.* 1995, p. 319.

[88] Rappole 1995, p. 146.

[89] Noss and Peters 1995, p. viii.

[90] *Ibid.*

[91] A particularly persuasive argument for a bottleneck for migrant populations in their nonbreeding grounds is made by John Rappole (1995), pp. 147-150. Eleven species with a South American affinity are among the neotropical migrants that Rappole judges most likely to decline in the near future. The populations of the following eight species of this group appear to be limited by factors on the nonbreeding grounds: buff-breasted sandpiper, black-billed cuckoo, veery, gray-cheeked thrush, yellow-green vireo, bay-breasted warbler, cerulean warbler, and Connecticut warbler.

[92] The ecoregion approach is appropriate for evaluating the broad distribution of neotropical migratory birds in the ASC Region. The size of ecoregion units, however, and the fact that their characterization is based on pre-colonization conditions do not allow for evaluation of local and more recent habitat patterns. Lacking a suitable land classification scheme, therefore, we were unable to map patterns of aquatic habitats and human-altered (secondary, disturbed) habitats in order to examine their relationship to the distribution of neotropical migrants. The Florida and Caribbean Marine Conservation Science Center of The Nature Conservancy is currently developing marine ecoregions. The Nature Conservancy would like to expand this kind of study.

[93] Storm-petrels are pelagic species, but pelagic is not included in our aquatic category.

[94] Rappole 1995, pp. 151-152.

[95] Ridgely and Tudor 1989, p. 21.

[96] Lynch 1989, p. 186.

[97] Rappole 1995, pp. 71-74.

[98] *Ibid.*, pp. 8, 9, 54, and 63.

[99] *Ibid.*, p. 189.

[100] Lynch 1989, p. 240.

[101] Kricher and Davis 1989, pp. 217-219.

[102] Robbins *et al.* 1989a, p. 21.

[103] Ridgely and Tudor 1989, p. 61. Although most research on plantations and migrants has been conducted in Central America and the Caribbean, we believe these data are probably applicable to the ASC Region as well, despite its different species composition and lower species diversity and density. Whether the high diversity occurs in plantations that are not adjacent to forest is unknown, but it is unlikely. Also, native species may be attracting migrants to these areas. In addition, a plantation's size may have a negative effect on bird occurrence. Many migrants are seen in small banana patches but not in large banana plantations. Accordingly to Robert Ridgely, large citrus plantations and banana groves in South America are almost "sterile" with respect to neotropical migratory birds.

[104] Wille 1994.

[105] Robbins *et al.* 1989a, p. 218.

[106] *Ibid.*

[107] Rappole 1995, pp. 9-27.

[108] Robbins *et al.* 1989a, p. 217.

[109] Morton 1989, p. 583.

[110] Robbins *et al.* 1989c, p. 7661.

[111] Dinerstein *et al.* 1995, pp. 49-58.

[112] Not included are mangrove designations.

[113] Hilty pers. comm. 1995.

[114] Dinerstein *et al.* 1995.

[115] Ridgely and Tudor 1989.

[116] Dinerstein *et al.* 1995.

[117] *Ibid.*

[118] *Ibid.*

[119] *Ibid.*

[120] *Ibid.*

[121] *Ibid.*

[122] *Ibid.*

[123] *Ibid.*

[124] *Ibid.*

[125] *Ibid.*

[126] *Ibid.*

[127] *Ibid.*

[128] Ridgely and Tudor 1989.

[129] *Ibid.*

[130] Dinerstein *et al.* 1995.

[131] *Ibid.*

[132] *Ibid.*